A USER'S GUIDE TO THE USA PATRIOT ACT AND BEYOND

Robert P. Abele

University Press of America,® Inc.

Lanham · Boulder · New York · Toronto · Oxford

⊖™ The paper used in this publication meets the minimum
requirements of American National Standard for Information
Sciences—Permanence of Paper for Printed Library Materials,
ANSI Z39.48—1984

To Sue

TABLE OF CONTENTS

Preface

In the panicked and grief-stricken first few months after the horrific events of September 11, 2001, a small group of people within the Bush administration sought to take full advantage of the fear and terror of the moment by pushing legislation through Congress that vastly expanded governmental power and radically truncated the civil rights of the citizens of the United States. So say the civil libertarians who have read the USA PATRIOT Act and the other pieces of legislation being drafted by the Bush administration and other Congressional leaders. These people are concerned that Congress in general and the Bush administration in particular are attempting to use the fear generated by 9/11 in order to further a narrow agenda of power consolidation by upper-level government officials, at the expense of the rights guaranteed by our Constitution which we hold as such an integral part of our democracy.

Count this author as one of those who is deeply concerned about fundamental civil liberties being undermined by various legislations such as the USA PATRIOT Act, the so-called "Victory Act," and the proposal by Attorney General John Ashcroft entitled "The Domestic Security Enhancement Act of 2003," nicknamed "Patriot II." These Acts give broad and sweeping powers to the Federal government in its ability to collect information of all kinds on citizens and foreign nationals of the United States. Beyond that, the legal authority it gives to our government to operate in complete secrecy, along with the power given to the Justice Department to arrest and detain foreign nationals, are stunning in their scope. While the government claims that such powers and actions are necessary in the fight against terrorism, even a superficial reading of the acts of legislation outlined in this book will give lie to this official position of our government officials.

Specifically, this book will examine the Foreign Intelligence Surveillance Act (FISA, 1978), the USA PATRIOT Act, the Domestic Security Enhancement Act of 2003, and other legislative proposals made in the months and year following the horrendous events of 9/11/01. The reason for such an investigation is simply to present to the intelligent reader the salient points of each legislative proposal, to bookend them by an examination of the philosophical underpinnings of

our great Bill of Rights, and to analyze from the perspective of the Bill
of Rights the legislation that is now either the law of the land, or is
about to be proposed as law. At least until the fourth chapter, I have attempted to allow the reader to exercise his/her own judgment
concerning whether or not these Acts of Congress can peacefully coex-
ist with the Bill of Rights. My own conclusions will be apparent
enough in Chapter Four, in which I present both a summary of analyses
by the ACLU and other civil liberties groups and persons, as well as
my own analysis. Whatever conclusion one draws about USA
PATRIOT and its siblings, no one who knows the content of the Act(s)
can help but conclude that this is a very critical and urgent time for
American democracy. It is not at all an exaggeration to claim that the
civil liberties of the citizens of America are at least threatened if not
truncated by the USA PATRIOT Act, and many of these rights certainly are completely overrun in "Patriot II." It is the purpose of this
book to inform the reader as to what is happening in as nontechnical a
manner as possible. Since the concern of this text is with civil rights
under PATRIOT and its successors, attention will not be given to those
sections of the PATRIOT Act that do not touch upon such rights. For
example, the Act guarantees governmental support of the families of
persons killed in terrorist attacks. Since this neither detracts from nor
reinforces civil rights, it will not be detailed here. The same is true with
other provisions of PATRIOT which are innocuous regarding civil liberties. With this in mind, an outline of the main issues in this book may
now be presented.

Chapter One presents the philosophical underpinnings of our
Bill of Rights as seen in the philosophy of John Locke. This is what
will be referred to as "the spirit of the law," since it presents the phi-
losophical/intellectual grounding of what became the U.S. Bill of
Rights. While Locke receives the most attention in this chapter, there
are also references made to other very important influences in the development of the Bill of Rights in the U.S. Constitution. These influences include such things as the Magna Carta, The Bill of Rights in
England, and Common Law tradition of England, to name just a few.

Chapter Two presents the main points of the Foreign Intelligence Surveillance Act of 1978 (FISA), the law that the PATRIOT Act
is intended to "update." This chapter compares FISA with the main issues involved in the USA PATRIOT Act. The latter, of course, receives
most of the attention in this chapter.

In Chapter Three I present a summary of the legislation currently before Congress or forthcoming. This chapter includes an examination of the proposal of the Justice Department entitled "The Do-

mestic Security Enhancement Act of 2003," otherwise known by its nickname, "PATRIOT II." It is followed, in Chapter Four, by a summary of some of the more important and interesting analyses of USA PATRIOT, along with some thoughts of my own concerning the Act. Chapter Five closes this book with the latest news and developments related to the PATRIOT Act and its relatives as of the end of the year 2003, along with some final reflections.

There are numerous people whose assistance has been immensely valuable in writing this text. First of all, Ms. Kim Radek, my colleague in the Humanities Department at Illinois Valley Community College, first prodded me to do this research for a talk at our college concerning what, if anything, had changed since 9/11. It was my preparation for that talk that started me down the road to writing this text. Finally, Ms. Joey Jordan was not only an invaluable support throughout the project, but provided me an outlet for my research in California public radio.

Chapter One: Our Rights Tradition: From the English Tradition to John Locke to the Bill of Rights

If the USA PATRIOT ACT in fact undermines our basic rights, it is imperative that we understand exactly what those rights are and how they came to play such an important part of our democratic tradition in the United States. The purpose of this chapter is to present a brief historico-philosophical overview of the rights tradition in western thought and jurisprudence, ending with an examination of the Bill of Rights. The point of doing this is to provide a foundation and a point of comparison between the rights tradition of the United States and the PATRIOT Act. We will look to present both the "spirit" and the "law" of the principles to which we pledge our allegiance as citizens of the United States.

I. The English Tradition that Gave Birth to the U.S. Bill of Rights

Our own Bill of Rights did not come into being suddenly and from an intellectual vacuum. Rather, there were two profound influences on the rights tradition in the United States. The first was the series of developments that took place in English society between 1215 and 1690. The second was the philosophy of John Locke, whose impact on Thomas Jefferson and the writers of the Bill of Rights was profound. We will begin with the English jurisprudential tradition, and the changes to it that eventually gave birth to a rights tradition.

We begin with a summary of the important developments that occurred in the English legal tradition, beginning with the Magna Carta ("Great Charter") of 1215. This interesting document, signed by King John of England, established the right to trial by jury, the right to due process of law, and the principle that the power of the monarchy was not absolute. It is the due process clause of the Magna Carta that became the Fifth Amendment to our Constitution, which is examined below.

The Petition of Right was created in 1628, with the aim of forbidding the king from arresting people arbitrarily, from housing soldiers in citizen homes without their consent, and from holding that the king is above the rule of law. Of primary concern here were the trials of citizens by the military, the arrest and imprisonment of citizens without cause or on fiat from the king or other authorities, taxation without Parliamentary consent, and self-incrimination.[1] This later becomes the concern for "probable cause" of the Fourth Amendment and the right against self-incrimination of the Fifth Amendment to the U.S. Constitution.

The right of Habeas Corpus (literally "have the body") is the right of an arrested or detained person to be brought before a court of law to decide on the legality of his/her detention or imprisonment. This right, in essence, is one against the government. It forces the government holding the person to go to court and prove that the detained person is being detained legally. The purpose of this right is "to prevent illegal arrests and unlawful imprisonments."[2] The concerns of habeas corpus, among others, led to the Eighth Amendment to the U.S. Constitution.

The English Bill of Rights of 1689 listed among them several rights that were taken over by the writers of the U.S. Constitution, among them the right to petition the king (U.S. First Amendment), the right to bear arms (U.S. Second Amendment), the prohibition of excessive bails and fines and cruel and unusual punishment (U.S. Eighth Amendment).

The stage is now set for the first full, democratic philosophy of human rights. John Locke (1632-1704) was an English native, whose father was an attorney for Parliament. In 1667 Locke, together with Lord Ashley, Earl of Shaftesbury, wrote the Constitution for the new American colony of North Carolina. His most famous work, the one of interest to the rights tradition in America, is entitled *Two Treatises of Government*, and was published in 1690. In this work, Locke sets out what he considers to be the main rights of human beings, based on the fact that they were humans. He called this "natural law." His theory was tremendously influential on the founders of the young United States of America, particularly on Thomas Jefferson, John Adams, James Madison, and George Mason. Most specifically, Locke's ideas gave birth, through Jefferson, to the Declaration of Independence of the United States. It is well, then, that we take some time to study Locke thoroughly in order to understand that conceptual pillars that support our Declaration of Independence and the Bill of Rights of the U.S. Constitution.

Locke begins his discussion of human rights by referring to a "state of nature," within which exists a "law of nature." The "law of nature" is our reason, by which we determine what is right and wrong, and it is our reason that makes us free. Thus, the ability we each have to determine our actions, without being compelled to do so by others, is founded on the fact that humans possess reason:

> The Freedom then of Man and Liberty of acting according to his own Will, is grounded on his having Reason which is able to instruct him in that Law he is to govern himself by, and make him know how far he is left to the freedom of his own will.[3]

Thus, because the law of nature is reason, Locke can define the law as the liberty of acting according to our own will, and not from the force of others. It is our reason that must control all our actions (II, 8), and it is reason that places us above animals (II, 58). Perhaps most important for Locke, reason is the structure of mutual cooperation in a society:

> So that the end and measure of this Power, when in every Man's hands in the state of Nature, being the preservation of all of his Society, that is, all Mankind in general, it can have no other end or measure, when in the hands of the Magistrate, but to preserve the Members of that Society in their Lives, Liberties, and Possessions.[4]

Thus, reason is that power "which God hath given to be the Rule betwixt Man and Man, and the common bond whereby humane kind is united into one fellowship and societie." Furthermore, any person who attempts to get another person into his or her power/under his or her will, denies that reason is the rule between humans, and thus "becomes liable to be destroyed by the injured person and the rest of mankind, as any other wild beast."[5] Any law of society must be created in reference to this standard of reason:

> Law is . . . not so much the limitation as the direction of a free and intelligent agent to his own proper interest." Thus, "the end of law is not to abolish or restrain, but to preserve and enlarge freedom.[6]

But if reason is the rule, what exactly does reason tell us to do? Most importantly for Locke, reason dictates that no one ought to harm another in his life, health, liberty or possessions (II, 6). This means, for Locke, not simply egoistic self-preservation, but that the dictate of reason requires us to preserve all of humanity, where our own preservation does not conflict with this principle. (II, 6) This principle of reason can be discovered even when one is not bound by a civil society. This "unbound" condition Locke refers to as "the state of nature," that is, a state outside of a politically organized society.

The state of nature characterizes the condition of people *qua* individuals; that is, in a state where no organized community exists. In such a state, people by nature are in "a state of perfect freedom to order their actions, possessions, and persons as they think fit." (II, 4) Moreover, "he who would take away [my] freedom declares war on me. Freedom is the fence to [my preservation], because to take away freedom is to imply that one wants to take away everything else, freedom being the foundation of all the rest." (II, 17) Freedom is such a foundational trait of humans that

> This freedom from Absolute, Arbitrary Power, is so necessary to, and closely joyned with a Man's Preservation, that he cannot part with it, but by what forfeits his Preservation and Life together. (II, 23)

In addition to freedom, humans are naturally free and naturally equal. Locke defines the "state of equality" as a condition in which no one has more (political) power than another (i.e., no one has more power *over* another). The state of liberty is to be free "not to be under the Will or Legislative Authority of Man, but to have only the Law of Nature for his Rule." (II, 22) This liberty is "not a state of license;" rather it is a limited state of liberty due to reason, in which no one possesses the liberty to destroy oneself or any other creature beyond what preservation calls for. (II, 6)

Since our natural state as humans is to be rational, free, and equal in social power, this results in two distinct rights in the state of nature: the right of self-preservation and the preservation of all humanity, and the right to punish wrongdoers. (II, 11, 18, 19).

Given all this wonderful freedom and individuality, why would we ever want to join up and form a society? For Locke, the reasons are twofold. First, because we are naturally inclined not to be alone (the reason we have understanding and language to begin with, according to Locke) (II, 77); second, for the purpose of punishing those who violate the natural law.

> But because no Political Society can be nor subsist without having in it self the Power to preserve the Property, and in order thereunto punish the Offences of all those of that Society; there, and there only is Political Society, where every one of the Members hath quitted this natural Power, re-

sign'd it up into the hands of the Community in all cases
that exclude him not from appealing for Protection to the
Law established by it.[7]

We thus begin our transition into the reason for a political society: "for [our] comfortable, safe, and peaceable living one amongst
another, in a secure enjoyment of [our] properties, and a greater Security against any that are not of it." (II, 95, p. 330-1) Locke refers to this
development whereby we form communities or governments for our
protection, as "the social compact." It is a relationship of "trust" between people and the government they form. This trust is necessary to
make democracy work.(II, 107), as the government is the "deputy" of
the people, who can be replaced if they abuse the trust the people put in
them. (II, 240; 8). Also, this trust means that the government is not only
established by such trust, but is only a legitimate government when the
people, together, have decided to so lend their trust to it. This is what
Locke calls the consent of the governed (II, 8, 95-98). Finally, it is the
people who determine when their trust has been broken by the government, for only the people who turn over their powers can claim its
abuse (II, 240, 5-7). This argues for not only the possibility of constitutional and governmental change, but also for revolution: "Governments
are dissolved . . . when the Legislative . . . acts contrary to their
'Trust.'" (II, 221, 2-5).

If we take all of this into account in forming the basis for political organization, we may conclude with Locke that the real origin of
society is the protection of "property." Property has a specific and
unique definition in Locke; it includes our "lives, liberties, and estates"
(II, 9, 123). Furthermore, "every man has a property in his own person." Thus, Locke gives two definitions of property. The main one,
used most often, is the former, which includes the idea that one can
make his/her own what is not already possessed by another. But in re-
gards to this idea there is an interesting limit Locke puts on acquisition
of property. One is not permitted, according to the law of nature, to
take as much property as he wants, only that which he can make use of
for self-preservation, and before it spoils (II, 5, 30), and it must not be
wasted (II, 5, 36).

Locke uses both definitions of property in his answer to the
question concerning why we come together in society: "the great and
chief end . . . of mens uniting into Commonwealths, and putting of
themselves under government, is the preservation of their property."
(II, 9, 124) But property has this nature, that "without a man's [sic.]
own consent it cannot be taken away form him" (II, 193)

The governing body that results from this coming together is created by a partial surrender of the natural rights to preservation of humanity and to a full surrender of the right to punish wrongdoers. Thus the power of government in Locke consists solely in the function of preserving the "lives, liberties and estates" of those who consent to it by surrendering their full rights from the state of nature. This means that the legislative may not take any part of a person's property without their consent, for such preservation is why the government is formed to begin with (II, 11, 138). When the rights of self-preservation of the whole and of punishment are surrendered to society in the form of the legislative, the power of the latter can never be extended beyond the common good (II, 9, 123; 128-31). Thus, the first law governing the legislative is "the preservation of society and...the public good of every person in it" (II, 11, 134). This is why the consent of society is necessary for the existence and proper function of the legislative. Thus the power of the legislative, "in the utmost bounds of it, is limited to the public good of the society . . . It is a power that has no right to destroy, enslave, or designedly impoverish the subjects."

But since our concern is with rights, what does Locke have to say on this subject? Locke never explicitly says what a right is; he is more concerned with the duties of government toward its people, and with the right-duty correlation of persons with regard to other individuals in a society. Furthermore, he tends to use synonyms for rights, such as power, entitlement, title, privilege, claim, and liberty. His interest seems to be more on the issue of equal rights for all, regardless of what specific rights we all possess. Nevertheless, it is still possible to see a nascent theory of rights in Locke. It is perhaps best to let Locke speak for himself on what "rights" are, and build a general theory out of that. Some of the more important passages in which Locke discusses rights are the following:

Our natural condition is "a state of perfect freedom to order [our] actions, and dispose of [our] possessions, as [we] see fit." (II, 4)

We have "a liberty to follow [our] own will(s) in all things, where the rule prescribes not." (II, 22)

Our "uncontrollable liberty . . . to dispose of person or possessions" (II, 6) is in part a moral freedom to pursue our own life plan, independent of duty. Thus, we have a right not to be harmed or interfered with while pursuing our own "innocent ends" (II, 128; 190).

We all have a right to freedom from harm and interference by others, provided that our actions stay within the bound of natural law. This is what Locke calls "the freedom to our own person" (II, 190).

Are rights inalienable (i.e. can they be surrendered by their possessors)? Are rights absolute (i.e., no permissible infringement on any portion of a given right? If not, where does one draw the line)? These questions are difficult to answer, as Locke is generally silent on them. We may answer the first question by stating that although Locke does not mention the term "inalienable" in his writings, Lockean analysts are in general agreement that he does mean to hold that rights are inalienable.[8] We may answer the second question about the absoluteness of rights in Locke in several steps.[9]

First, in his *Essay on Toleration*, Locke does speak of rights as "absolute," in particular the right to "speculative opinion and divine worship." However, Locke also notes that, in a conflict of rights, one right is justifiably overridden by another (II, 183; 176; 230); that the value of preserving peace in society may sometimes override individual rights (176); and that consideration of the common good "limit and alter the obligation even of some of the laws of God" (183). Thus we may conclude that rights may not always be absolute for Locke, but they are almost absolute, the two main exceptions being the conflict of rights and extraordinary social cost in keeping rights absolute. So no one can rightfully use our body, mind, or labor without our consent (II, 27, 32, 190).

How might we conclude this discussion on the theory of government and human rights in Locke that so deeply influenced the founders of the governmental structure of the United States? Perhaps we may conclude, with A. John Simmons, a Lockean analyst, that humanity "is best preserved when it is left a large area of freedom . . . *regardless* of what (innocent) ends we choose to use our freedom to pursue."[10] The reason for this, says Simmons, is that for Locke humanity is best preserved when Natural Law is obeyed. We all have an equal right to freedom from harm and interference by others, provided that our actions stay within the bounds of Natural Law.[11] This is "the freedom to our own person" Locke speaks so highly of in his *Two Treatises* (II, 190).

II. Locke, Jefferson, and the Declaration of Independence

With the basic principles of Locke having been established, it is a very simple thing to see how deeply Locke influenced the writer of the Declaration of Independence, Thomas Jefferson. This section will simply point out those passages in the Declaration that were taken in whole or in part from the *Two Treatises* of Locke.

1) John Locke: "The State of Nature has a Law of Nature to govern it, which obliges every one: And Reason, which is that Law,

teaches all Mankind, who will but consult it, that being all equal and independent, no one ought to harm another."[12]

The Declaration of Independence: "We hold these truths to be self-evident."

2) John Locke: In the state of nature there is "a State also of Equality, wherein all the Power and Jurisdiction is reciprocal, no one having more than another: there being nothing more evident, than that Creatures of the same species and rank promiscuously born to all the same advantages of Nature."[13]

The Declaration of Independence: "that all men are created equal."

3) John Locke: "For Men being all the Workmanship of one Omnipotent, and infinitely wise Maker . . . ought . . . as much as he can, *to preserve the rest of Mankind*, and may not...impair the life, or what tends to the Preservation of the Life, the Liberty, Health, Limb or Goods of another."[14]

The Declaration of Independence: "that they are endowed by their Creator with certain unalienable rights."

4) John Locke: We unite with others "for the mutual preservation of [our] lives, liberties and estates, which I call by the general name, Property."[15]

The Declaration of Independence: "that among these are life, liberty, and the pursuit of happiness."

5) John Locke: In Chapters II, IX, and XI of the *Two Treatises*, Locke argues that all rights belong to humans by virtue of the fact that they are human, and thus such rights precede and supercede the power of government. Therefore, the extent of governmental power is limited by its obligation to secure the rights of the people,[16] which, for Locke, means "the preservation of Society, and . . . of every person in it." This requires "the consent of the Society, over whom no body can have a Power to make Laws, but by their own consent, and by Authority received from them."[17]

The Declaration of Independence: "That, to secure these rights, governments are instituted among men, deriving their just powers from the consent of the governed."

6) John Locke: "there remains still in the people a Supreme power to remove or alter the legislative, when they find the legislative act contrary to the trust reposed in them . . . whenever they [i.e. the legislative] shall be so foolish, or so wicked, as to lay and carry on designs against the liberties and properties of the subject."[18]

The Declaration of Independence: "that, whenever any form of government becomes destructive of these ends, it is the right of the people to alter or to abolish it."

7) John Locke: Revolt of the people becomes necessary "when a long train of abuses, prevarications, and artifices, all tending the same way, make the design visible to the people."[19]

The Declaration of Independence: "when a long train of abuses and usurpations . . . evinces a design to reduce them under absolute despotism, it is their right, it is their duty, to throw off such government and to provide new guards for their future security."

8) John Locke: The function and purpose of the legislature is to represent the public good.[20]

The Declaration of Independence: "the right of representation in the legislature."

These principles, intellectually formulated by Locke and practically applied by Jefferson, form the bedrock to the tradition of rights that are the pillars of our form of democracy.

III. The Bill of Rights of the Constitution of the United States

The Bill of Rights is the first ten amendments to the U.S. Constitution, which were ratified by the states in 1791. Whereas the Declaration of Independence lays out the principles of our rights, the Bill of Rights lays out the civil or legal rights we possess. The American people were leery of having rights simply set by principle, since such rights could easily be abused by ruling powers. As such, they were much more inclined to codify human rights in the Constitution in order to give them power as the law of the land. Therefore, as Supreme Court Justice Ruth Bader Ginsburg states, "the Bill of Rights *assumes* the existence of fundamental human rights—for example, freedom of speech, press, and assembly—and simply instructs states not to interfere with those rights."[21] Thus, the Bill of Rights is the legal instrument used by U.S. Courts today, being a combination of natural rights and legal rights. However, as we have seen, the Bill itself has its grounding in the Declaration of Independence, which has its grounding in the philosophy of John Locke. When all of these factors are known and taken into account, we will have succeeded in comprehending both the letter and the spirit of the Bill of Rights. The examination of the Bill of Rights to follow will focus only on those aspects of the Bill the understanding of which is necessary for developing a critique of the USA PATRIOT Act. There is, of course, a richness and depth to the Bill of Rights in the U.S. Constitution that far exceeds the treatment of it here.[22]

We begin, then, with the First Amendment to the U.S. Constitution, which reads as follows:

> Congress shall make no law respecting an establishment of religion, or prohibiting the free exercise thereof, or abridging the freedom of speech, or of the press, or the right of the people peaceably to assemble, and to petition the Government for a redress of grievances.

In addition to the stated rights contained in this amendment, the U.S. Supreme Court has ruled that "freedom of association" is included as a right protected by the First Amendment.[23] The rights to freedom of speech, press, assembly, and petition are called freedoms of expression. The Supreme Court has ruled over the years that included in the right to free speech are spoken words (e.g. debates and public meetings), speech combined with action (e.g. demonstrating and picketing), and the right not to speak.[24] The limits to this right of free speech include obscenity, defamation (abusive or insulting words in public and/or those that incite violence), fighting words, false commercial speech, and speech in special places (e.g. military bases, prisons, and schools, when speech disrupts the purpose of the facility).[25] Specifically, the Court has determined that one of three conditions must be met for the determination that free speech has gone too far, and requires legal punishment: 1) Clear and present danger of criminal action; 2) Advocacy of abstract doctrine (i.e. only action can be punished, not belief); 3) Imminent action (i.e. speech that incites an immediate lawless action [e.g. burning down the court house], not an illegal action in general [e.g. advocating government overthrow]).[26]

Included in the First amendment is the freedom of assembly, which includes peaceable assembly and freedom of association (i.e. freedom of people to join together for a common purpose or activity).[27]

We move to the Fourth Amendment, which says:

> The right of the people to be secure in their persons, houses, papers, and effects, against unreasonable searches and seizures, shall not be violated, and no Warrants shall issue, but upon probable cause, supported by Oath or affirmation, and particularly describing the place to be searched, and the persons or things to be seized.

This will be of crucial concern in our analysis of USA PATRIOT forthcoming. Requiring the government to produce probable cause for such activities protects the right against illegal searches and seizures. "Probable cause" means that the government must have some reason to believe that a criminal activity is taking place or about to take place, and that they are willing to swear an oath to that effect. This provision of law was a reaction against the practice of "general warrants" in England, carried over to America by British government, whereby a government official on any level could "search wherever they wanted and . . . seize whatever or whomever they wished."[28]

It is important to note that not all searches and seizures require warrants, and some do not even require probable cause. The Supreme Court decides each case individually, but their general principle is that warrantless searches or seizures, or those without probable cause, are unconstitutional.

Connected with the Fourth amendment is the right to privacy. Prior to 1890, Americans had only a vague notion of "privacy rights." The only court cases that upheld such rights concerned private property. This right included things as ruining a person's reputation because of the revelation of private details about his/her life.

However, the specific interpretation of human rights in the U.S. Constitution as including individual privacy was not brought forward until 1890, in an essay by Supreme Court Justices Lewis Brandeis and Samuel D. Warren. In this essay, they submit that there is a constitutional right "to be left alone," and that this right was self-evident. This philosophy was finally codified in the case *Olmstead v. U.S.*, in 1928. Justice Brandeis wrote the majority opinion:

> The right to be left alone—the most comprehensive of our rights, and the right most valued by civilized men [sic.] To protect that right, every unjustifiable intrusion by the government upon the privacy of the individual, whatever the means employed, must be deemed a violation of the Fourth Amendment.[29]

From there, the Court went on to apply and enforce this right to privacy in other decisions. For example, in *Griswold v. Connecticut* (1965), the Supreme Court ruled that a Connecticut statute forbidding the use of contraceptives violated the right to marital privacy. Again, in *Roe v. Wade* (1973), the right to privacy was violated by bans on abortions.

The Fifth Amendment to the Constitution does not concern us in its entirety, but only where "due process of law" is concerned. Here is the entire Amendment:

> No person shall be held to answer for a capital, or otherwise infamous crime, unless on a presentment or indictment of a grand jury, except in cases arising in the land or naval forces, or in the Militia, when in actual service in time of War or public danger; nor shall any person be subject for the same offense to be twice put in jeopardy of life or limb; nor shall be compelled in any criminal case, to be a witness against himself, nor be deprived of life, liberty, or property, without due process of law; nor shall private property be taken for public use without just compensation.

There are three issues here that concern us in examining the USA PATRIOT Act: the right to a grand jury for capital crimes; the right against self-incrimination; the right to due process of law.

The right to grand jury indictment is the right of a person to have a jury composed of other citizens examine the evidence that a prosecutor has collected, in order to determine whether or not the prosecutor has evidence sufficient enough to order a trial for a given person. It applies only to the federal government, and is conducted ex parte (i.e. only the prosecutor is present). The proceedings of a grand jury are secret. These proceedings are conducted for capital crimes (i.e. crimes which carry a sentence of death upon conviction).

The right against self-incrimination requires the government to present enough evidence to prove its case without coercing or requiring a confession on the part of the accused. The maxim of this part of the Fifth Amendment is that one is presumed innocent until proven guilty. This "applies to any government proceeding, criminal or civil, in which a person is forced to answer a question."[30] According to Linda Monk, a constitutional lawyer and author of *The Bill of Rights: A User's Guide*, the Fifth Amendment

> does not prohibit the government from requiring a defendant to provide nontestimonial evidence—such as fingerprints, handwriting samples, fingernail clippings, and blood specimens. This type of evidence is considered physical evidence, rather than testimony.[31]

We come next to the very important "due process" clause of the Fifth Amendment. "Due process" is the norm that states that the government must follow fair and non-arbitrary rules in its conduct toward its citizens, particularly in a court of law. According to Monk, there are two types of due process: procedural and substantive. Procedural due process requires that the way laws are enforced by government officials must be fair, while substantive due process requires that the laws themselves be fair.[32] Part of the procedural rules requires that the government prove its case beyond a reasonable doubt before punitive action is undertaken.

The Sixth Amendment states that

> In all criminal prosecutions, the accused shall enjoy the right to a speedy and public trial, by an impartial jury of the State and district wherein the crime shall have been committed; which district shall have been preciously ascertained by law, and to be informed of the nature and cause of the accusation; to be confronted with the witnesses against him; to have compulsory process for obtaining witnesses in his favor, and to have the assistance of counsel for his defense.

Article III of the Constitution states that "the trial of all crimes, except in cases of impeachment, shall be by jury." Perhaps prophetically, Linda Monk makes the following query:

> what if the government could postpone trial for years, or prosecute the accused in secret, or exclude women from the jury, or refuse to tell the accused the charges, or allow witnesses to make accusations secretly? What if only the government could force witnesses to testify or use lawyers?[33]

This inquiry might be something worth remembering as we examine the PATRIOT Acts I and II. For now, though, the focus is on the Sixth Amendment alone, the point of which is to provide those who are accused by the government of a crime, a fair and equal chance to defend themselves in court, in the face of overwhelming governmental power and resources to fund their own case. We will detail these specific rights as follows.

First, "the right to a speedy and public trial" is intended to guarantee several things, such as the presumption of innocence, prevention of long periods of imprisonment for the accused, and the accuracy of evidence, which insures the fairness of verdict. In the Speedy Trial

Act of 1974, Congress set the beginning of a trial date for federal trials
to be no more than 100 days after an arrest. The Supreme Court, however, seems to rule more on a case-by-case basis regarding the definition of "speedy" trial.[34]

The Sixth Amendment likewise guarantees the right to a public trial. The purpose of this right is, again, to prevent government
abuse of a defendant and the process of trial by acting in secret. Not all
trials are required to be made public, however.

There is a right "to be informed of the nature and cause of the
accusation" stated by the Sixth Amendment, a right "to be confronted
with the witnesses against him," and a right "to have the assistance of
counsel for his defense." These are fairly self-explanatory, so only a
comment or two need be made here. The latter section requiring that
witnesses against a person be brought into the court of law is there so
that the defendant might hear the charges and cross-examine the witness. The right to counsel is a guarantee that the rights of the defendant,
which may be unknown to him/her, are as equally and fairly repre-
sented as is the case against him/her. This right applies from the moment police questioning begins.

Here is the Eighth Amendment to the Constitution:

> Excessive bail shall not be required, nor excessive fines
> imposed, nor cruel and unusual punishments inflicted.

The Supreme Court ruled in 1958 that the Eighth Amendment
"must draw its meaning from evolving standards of decency that mark
the progress of a maturing society."[35] Thus, punishments that were
common in the nineteenth century, such as whipping and drawing and
quartering, are not permissible today. While capital punishment remains a highly controversial issue under this Amendment, it is not the
intent to discuss this issue here. Generally, however, the Supreme Court
has consistently upheld the death penalty for capital crimes such as
murder, but not for other crimes.[36]

IV. Universalizing Our Rights Tradition: The United Nations Uni-versal Declaration of Human Rights

The spread of the importance of the rights tradition in western
culture perhaps hit a climax in 1948, with the passage of the United Nations "Universal Declaration of Human Rights." Here, for the first time
in history, we see the philosophy of John Locke brought to full fruition.
Here, too, we see the vision of the longest working Constitution in the

world, that of the United States, given world validation. The passage of this important document, signed by the United States, is truly a historic achievement of universal proportions, in that it says, for the first time, that such rights as expressed by Locke and codified in the U.S. Bill of Rights applied to each and every human in the world, regardless of race, nationality, or gender. We will state only the rights contained in this document which apply to our discussion of the USA PATRIOT Act. While it may be well argued that the United Nations is not domestic law, which is what the USA Patriot Act is, briefly examining the U.N. Declaration will enable us to see more clearly the spirit of the rights tradition in its full flowering. Since it is not in fact domestic law, we will state without comment the Articles that possibly concern our discussion.

Article 7 of the U.N. Declaration states: "All are equal before the law and are entitled without any discrimination to equal protection of the law. All are entitled to equal protection against any discrimination in violation of this Declaration and against any incitement to such discrimination."

Article 8: "Everyone has the right to an effective remedy by the competent national tribunals for acts violating the fundamental rights granted him by the constitution or law."

Article 9: "No one shall be subjected to arbitrary arrest, detention or exile."

Article 10: "Everyone is entitled in full equality to a fair and public hearing by an independent and impartial tribunal, in the determination of his rights and obligations and of any criminal charge against him."

Article 12: "No one shall be subjected to arbitrary interference with his privacy, family, home or correspondence, nor to attacks upon his honour and reputation. Everyone has the right to protection of the law against such interference or attacks."

Article 18: "Everyone has the right to freedom of thought, conscience and religion; this right includes freedom to change his religion or belief, and freedom, either alone or in community with others and in public or private, to manifest his religion or belief in teaching, practice, worship and observance."

Article 19: "Everyone has the right to freedom of opinion and expression; this right includes freedom to hold opinions without interference and to seek, receive and impart information and ideas through any media and regardless of frontiers."

Many of the Articles contained in the Universal Declaration sound strikingly like the U.S. Bill of Rights. Perhaps that is due to the strong influence of Eleanor Roosevelt in the passage of the Declaration. Whatever the reason for the resemblance, it is important to keep in mind that the United States had a major role in drafting and passing this Declaration, and signed off on it, promising to uphold its Articles.

Having examined the letter and the spirit of human rights in brief, we are now in a much stronger position to examine and to critically evaluate the USA PATRIOT Act and other proposed legislation affecting the rights of the citizens and residents of the United States.

Notes

1 See Leonard W. Levy, *Origins of the Bill of Rights* (New Haven: Yale University Press, 1999), 4-5.

2 Monk, Linda. *The Bill of Rights: A User's Guide* (Close Up Foundation, 1991), 237.

3 Locke, John. *Two Treatises of Government* (Great Britain: Cambridge University Press, 1991), Second Essay, paragraph 63, 309.

4 Ibid., paragraph 172, 382.

5 Ibid.

6 Ibid., paragraph 57, 305-306.

7 Ibid., paragraph 87, 324.

8 For more on this, see A. John Simmons, *The Lockean Theory of Rights* (Princeton: Princeton University Press, 1992); Tuck, Richard, *Natural Rights* (Cambridge: Cambridge University Press, 1979); Shapiro, Ian. *The Evolution of Rights in Liberal Theory* (Cambridge: Cambridge University Press, 1986).

9 The following analysis is based on Simmons, *The Lockean Theory of Rights*, 90-94.

10 Simmons, ibid, 78.

11 Ibid.

12 Locke, *Two Treatises*, Book II, Chapter, II, paragraph 6.

13 Ibid., paragraph 4.

14 Ibid., paragraph 6.

15 Ibid., Chapter 9, paragraph 123.

16 See especially ibid. paragraph 131.

17 Ibid., paragraph 134.

18 Ibid., Chapter XIII, paragraph 149.

19 Ibid., Chapter XIX, paragraph 225.

20 Ibid., Chapters IX and XI, *passim*.

21 Monk, *The Bill of Rights*, 7 (emphasis mine).

22 Unless otherwise noted, the analysis that follows of the Bill of Rights is taken either from Monk, ibid., or from Monk, *The Words We Live By: Your Annotated Guide to the Constitution* (New York: Hyperion Press, 2003).

23 Ibid., p. 41.

24 For more detail on this, see Monk, *The Bill of Rights*, 62-67.

25 For more, see Monk, ibid., 67-74

26 Ibid., 73.

27 Ibid., 85.

28 Ibid., 104.

29 http://www.righttoprivacy.com.

30 Monk, *The Bill of Rights*, 127.

31 Ibid., 127.

32 Ibid., 128-132.

33 Ibid., 137.

34 See Monk, 140.

35 Quoted in Monk, 172.

36 For a thorough argument concerning the applicability of the Bill of Rights to non-citizens living in the United States, see David Cole, *Enemy Aliens* (New York: The New Press, 2003), Chapter 14, "The Bill of Rights as Human Rights," 210-227.

Chapter Two
The Foreign Intelligence Surveillance Act of 1978 and the USA PATRIOT Act

One of the most significant steps the federal government undertook to fight against terrorism prior to 9/11 was to pass the Foreign Intelligence Surveillance Act (FISA) in 1978. This Act allows the U.S. government to spy on foreign governments and foreign nationals. It prescribes procedures for requesting judicial authorization for electronic surveillance and physical searches of persons engaged in espionage or international terrorism against the U.S. on behalf of a foreign power. The first part of this chapter will review the important terms and procedures defined by FISA. This is not in any way intended to be a thorough or complete examination of the content of FISA. Rather, the purpose of reviewing FISA is to gain some background information that will assist us in locating the PATRIOT Act in the context of the fight of the United States against terrorism. After summarizing some of the main provisions of FISA, we will preview some of the significant differences between FISA and the USA PATRIOT Act. Finally, we will examine the significant provisions of the PATRIOT Act that have greatly concerned civil libertarians.

I. FISA Definitions

In Title 50, Chapter 36, Subchapter I, Section 1801, there are at least four notable terms that define the people and procedures involved in surveillance. These are:

1. "Foreign power:" defined as any "group engaged in international terrorism or activities in preparation therefore [sic.]."

2. "Agent of a foreign power:" "any person other than a U.S. person, who acts in the U.S. as an officer or employee of a foreign power."

3. "Minimization procedures:" "specific procedures, which shall be adopted by the Attorney General . . . to minimize the acquisition and retention, and prohibit the dissemination, of nonpublicly available information concerning unconsenting U.S. person . . . [N]o contents of any communication to which a U.S. person is a party shall be disclosed, disseminated, or used for any purpose or retained for longer than twenty-four hours."

4. "United States person means a citizen of the U.S., an alien lawfully admitted for permanent residence."

With regard to who may be spied on under FISA, Section 1802 allows for collection of foreign intelligence information "for periods of up to one year" if the Attorney General "certifies in writing that the electronic surveillance is aimed solely at the acquisition of the contents of communications transmitted . . . exclusively between or among foreign powers . . . *and there is no substantial likelihood that the surveillance will acquire the contents of any communication to which a U.S. person is a party"* (emphasis mine). This same section places the Attorney General under the supervision of the House Permanent Select Committee on Intelligence and the Senate Select Committee on Intelligence, to which he is required to report with his assessment of compliance with the procedures set by the Act.

II. What FISA Allows the Feds to Do

One of the most cherished traditions in American jurisprudence is the notion that probable cause is required before an agent of the federal government may eavesdrop on persons. The Act is specific regarding the requirements of probable cause and the use of warrant for electronic foreign surveillance. In Section 1805, not only is probable cause for spying required, but the Act is careful to ensure that only foreign agents are wiretapped, not citizens of the United States. Furthermore, any order approving electronic surveillance of foreigners

> shall specify the identity, if known, or a description of the
> target of the electronic surveillance; the nature and location
> of each of the facilities or places at which the electronic
> surveillance will be directed, if known; the type of informa-
> tion sought . . . the means by which the electronic surveil-
> lance will be effected and whether physical entry will be
> used to effect the surveillance; the period of time during
> which the electronic surveillance is approved; and when-
> ever more than one electronic, mechanical, or other surveil-
> lance device is to be used under the order.

Such surveillance activities may take place from ninety days to one year, but no longer than a year. In fact, FISA requires an extension of an original order for surveillance beyond the allotted time of ninety days to a year. According to FISA, each April the Attorney General must report to Congress on the total number of applications made for such orders, and the extensions approved for foreign spying.

Another issue the Act addresses concerns the use of physical searches for foreign intelligence gathering. Section 1822 of FISA allows such searches, even without warrant, if the Attorney General certifies in writing that "the physical search is solely directed at premises, information, material, or property used exclusively by, or under the open and exclusive control of, a foreign power or powers." Once again, however, FISA is careful to protect American persons, as there must be "no substantial likelihood that the physical search will involve the premises, information, material, or property of a U.S. person." The Attorney General is required to report to Congress on the use of these procedures every six months.

Section 1825 of FISA specifies several types and limits on actions a federal agent may take regarding electronic surveillance. First of all, this section allows information that is gained from a physical search concerning a U.S. person to be shared between Federal officers and employees, without the consent of the person, provided the minimization procedures are adhered to. Even here, however, there is an explicit requirement that no information gathered shall be disclosed "unless such disclosure is accompanied by a statement that such information...may only be used in a criminal proceeding." Furthermore, any person against whom information is obtained through a search "may move to suppress that evidence . . . on the grounds that the information was unlawfully acquired." Thus there are safeguards built into FISA procedures to protect the target of spying against possible abuses by government.

Note that, according to Section 1825, even when federal agents collect information through physical searches, FISA specifically requires that a notice of the search without court order be given to the person "after the Attorney General has determined there is no national security interest involved." In other words, the target of physical searches must be notified that a search has taken place.

In Section 1826 the Attorney General is again required to present a detailed report to Congress concerning

> all physical searches conducted pursuant to this subchapter . . . the total number of applications made for such orders approving physical searches under this subchapter; the total number of such orders either granted, modified, or denied; and the number of physical searches which involved searches of the residences, offices, or personal property of the U.S. persons.

Again, there is an overriding concern in FISA to protect U.S. persons against abuse of governmental spying power. In fact, the guiding phrase of FISA on governmental spying seems to be: "not concerning U.S. persons." This limitation on governmental surveillance is written throughout the FISA legislation.

It is in this chapter of FISA that we first meet with the power granted to the Attorney General to engage in what are called "pen registers" and "trap and trace devices." A pen register is a device used to record all numbers dialed from the telephone of the target of an investigation. A trap and trace device is one that records the source of any incoming call to a given phone number. Section 1842 of FISA allows the Attorney General to authorize such orders, even for U.S. persons, but only in order to obtain foreign intelligence information. No investigation of any U.S. person is permitted "solely on the basis of activities protected by the first amendment to the Constitution." Thus, FISA in fact allows the government to spy on American citizens if, and only if, the sole purpose of the spying is to collect foreign intelligence information. Note, though, the protections built into this allowance. Any order that allows such electronic eavesdropping must specify

> the identity, if known, of the person who is the subject of the investigation; the identity, if known, of the person to whom is leased or in whose name is listed the telephone line or other facility to which the pen register or trap and trace device is to be attached or applied; the attributes of the communications to which the order applies, such as the number or other identifier, and, if known, the location of the telephone line or other facility to which the pen register or trap and trace device is to be attached or applied.

Finally, this section places a gag order on landlords, custodians, and other persons who know of the existence of such devices installed on a target's telephone. The time limit for such conduct is "not to exceed 90 days."

At this point, we can see that FISA, while intended for foreign intelligence electronic eavesdropping, does in fact allow encroachment into the privacy of U.S. persons for the sole purpose of collecting foreign intelligence information. This information is an important factor in determining whether or not the PATRIOT Act goes too far regarding encroachment of civil liberties.

III. H.R. 3162: "Uniting and Strengthening America by Providing Appropriate Tools Required to Intercept and Obstruct Terrorism," a.k.a. "The USA PATRIOT Act"

Given what we have just reviewed from the Foreign Intelligence Surveillance Act, we are in a position to preview the changes PATRIOT makes to FISA. Perhaps the most critical change is that the allowances of government spying in FISA are now aimed directly at U.S. persons, whereas in FISA, as we have seen, there had been a consistent attempt to protect U.S. persons from such surveillance. With PATRIOT, such spying on American citizens can become much more common practice. Not only that, but there are certain jurisprudential changes made between FISA and PATRIOT. They include the following notions. The target of electronic surveillance in FISA was a "foreign agent;" in PATRIOT it becomes "any U.S. person." In addition, "terrorist activity," the central point of surveillance under FISA, becomes in PATRIOT "any domestic criminal activity." Perhaps alarmingly, the probable cause concerns of FISA are dismissed entirely in PATRIOT, and "suspicion" replaces probable cause. The point of FISA was to allow electronic surveillance for the purpose of prosecution; in PATRIOT, the point of surveillance becomes information gathering. Further, such information gathering is given a wide berth under PATRIOT. Whereas FISA had strict parameters requiring judicial oversight and reporting to Congress, PATRIOT substantially reduces Justice Department accountability. Finally, under PATRIOT, immigration policy is changed. Under PATRIOT, the Attorney General can deport foreign nationals on the basis of their speech or association with any group Ashcroft blacklists, without the Attorney General's showing that they are dangerous or a flight risk (the only two constitutionally recognized justifications for preventive detention).[1]

What follows will not be a complete or detailed examination of each section of the USA PATRIOT Act. The text itself is 342 pages in length, not all of which is threatening to civil rights in America. The parts of PATRIOT that cause civil rights concerns will be the ones that are highlighted here.

Congress passed the PATRIOT ACT on October 26, 2001, in response to the September 11 attacks on the World Trade Center and the Pentagon. Divided into Ten "Titles," the Act has as its goal the strengthening of the government's ability to combat terrorism.[2] The Act passed by an overwhelming margin (House vote: 356-66; Senate vote: 98-1, with the sole dissenting vote cast by Senator Russell Feingold of Wisconsin). As we shall see, there is some controversy surrounding this vote, as some Congressional representatives charged that they were unable to read it before it passed, and/or accused the Justice Department of underhanded manipulation to get this bill passed.[3] Furthermore, many of the provisions that are in PATRIOT were written prior to 9/11/01, and had been flatly rejected by Congress.[4] One way or another, it is now the law of the land, and it is the purpose of this section to examine the most noteworthy parts from the perspective of civil rights. While a number of the provisions have expiration or "sunset" dates of December 31, 2005, any investigation that started prior to this date under PATRIOT will be exempt from the sunset date.[5]

Title I: "Enhancing Domestic Security Against Terrorism."
     Among other things, this Title dramatically increases the funding for various agencies of the federal government, and expands electronic surveillance capabilities. Section 103, "Increased Funding for the Technical Support Center at the Federal Bureau of Investigation," adds much of the funding:

> to help meet the demands for activities to combat terrorism and support and enhance the tactical operations of the FBI, $200,000,000 for each of the fiscal years 2002, 2003, 2004.

     Section 105, Expansion of National Electronic Crime Task Force Initiative," adds the new electronic surveillance capabilities, by mandating the federal government to "develop a national network of electronic crime task forces . . . throughout the United States, for the purpose of preventing, detecting, and investigating various forms of electronic crimes."
     Section 106 of this Act, entitled "Presidential Authority," vastly expands the powers of the President beyond the International Emergency Powers Act. The IEPA allows the President to freeze the assets of a foreign nation or corporation involved with a threat to national security. Under PATRIOT, the President can now "confiscate any property" of "any foreign person, foreign organization, or foreign country" which he has determined has been involved in hostilities toward the United States.[6]

Title II: "Enhanced Surveillance Procedures"
     The first issue regarding the PATRIOT Act's possible violations of civil liberties is in this Title, which expands what information may be shared between agencies. This is especially noted in Sections 201 and 203. Section 201, entitled "Authority to Intercept Wire, Oral,

and Electronic Communications Relating to Terrorism," allows the FBI to do precisely what the title suggests. As C. William Michaels summarizes this section, this includes interception of all "forms of communication over any standard or cell phone, computer line, cable connection, or fax machine...That would include e-mails and any other communication over the Internet."[7]

Section 203 is entitled "Authority to Share Criminal Investigative Information," and authorizes

> Any investigative or law enforcement officer, or attorney for the Government, who by any means authorized by this chapter, has obtained knowledge of the contents of any wire, oral, or electronic communication, or evidence derived therefrom, may disclose such contents to any other Federal law enforcement, intelligence, protective immigration, national defense, or national security official to the extent that such contents include foreign intelligence.

In other words, any information gathered by any branch of the federal government may be shared with any other branch without court order and without the knowledge of the person whose information it is. In addition, there is no court order required for such information sharing. There is no sunset clause for this section.

Section 206 is entitled "Roving Surveillance Authority Under the Foreign Intelligence Surveillance Act of 1978." It amends FISA, which authorized phone taps of specified phones of the targets of investigations, limited to "foreign powers or agents," to add "roving wiretaps" (taps that are to be made to any phone or computer that a target of an intelligence gathering investigation might use), for any person.[8] It also excludes judges from monitoring whether the taps are being used as required by the court order.

We do not know how the Justice Department is using this section, because they say that the information contained under this section is "classified."[9]

The Constitutional issue here concerns the Fourth Amendment to the Constitution, which reads as follows:

> The right of the people to be secure in their persons, houses, papers, and effects, against unreasonable searches and seizures, shall not be violated, and no warrants shall issue, but upon probable cause, supported by oath or affirmation, and particularly describing the place to be searched, and the persons or things to be seized.

It would be well to keep this right in one's mind as one reads the content of the following sections of Title II.

Section 207, "Duration of FISA Surveillance of non-United States Persons who are Agents of a Foreign Power," allows orders for search warrants to be issued by a court for surveillance outside that court's jurisdiction. It also requires disclosure of records from phone companies and internet providers, should a government agent "request" such information from them. Section 207 has no sunset provision.

Section 209, "Seizure of Voice-mail Messages Pursuant to Warrants," allows the federal government to seize any voice mail message it wants to.

Section 213 of the Act is entitled "Authority of Delaying Notice of the Execution of a Warrant." It authorizes the search and seizure of any property, for any criminal offense, not just for causes related to terrorism, and permits a delay in the execution of a search warrant if the government finds "reasonable cause to believe that providing immediate notification of the execution of the warrant may have an adverse result." Thus, law enforcement authorities do not have to announce that they are looking for something or even what they are looking for; they can just show up at the home or office of a person, search and seize, and then tell that person later what they took and why they took it. Under Section 213, the authorities can delay notification for an unspecified "reasonable period." This section has no "sunset" clause.

There are some significant differences between this section of PATRIOT and FISA. For example, under the Fourth Amendment to the U.S. Constitution, police have to follow a "knock and announce" practice when entering a home or office. FISA changed this to allow "sneak and peak" searches exclusively where "foreign powers or their agents" were suspected of terrorism. PATRIOT not only suspends the "knock and announce principle," but in fact expands such actions and warrants to include "any criminal" investigation. Furthermore, it requires only that notice be given of a search or wiretap "within a reasonable period of its execution," which may be extended for "a good cause." As of October, 2003, The Department of Justice admits to having used Section 213 sixty-one times for the delay of execution of a warrant, and has requested and received 248 extensions of time for delaying such executions.[10]

Section 215 of Title II is entitled "Access to Records and Other Items Under the Foreign Intelligence Surveillance Act." It permits any Assistant Special Agent in Charge to obtain a court order "requiring the production of any tangible things (including books, records, papers, documents, and other items) for an investigation to protect against international terrorism or clandestine intelligence activities." There is no probable cause nor suspicion required for obtaining such information under Section 215. All that is required is an assertion that information is being sought for either terrorism or clandestine intelligence concerns. This section further requires a judge to "enter . . . [the] order as requested" if it meets the requirements of this section. The judge is permitted no discretion here regarding granting such permission for searches of a person's activities. Furthermore, this section forbids any person approached by the FBI from disclosing to any other person the fact that information was sought against another person. Perhaps most noteworthy here is that the practice is no longer relegated to such investigations of foreign nationals; USA PATRIOT here specifically uses the language "United States person," which includes regular U.S. citizens. Thus, any book or CD a person either purchases or borrows from a library is subject to government investigation and knowledge. Section 215 has a sunset date of 2005.

Sections 214 and 216: "Modification of Authorities Relating to use of Pen Registers and Trap and Trace Devices." Section 214 permits pen registers and "trap and trace devices" with no requirement of warrant for their use. All the government has to do is state that the intelligence gathering is "relevant to an ongoing terrorist investigation." "Pen registers" record all numbers dialed from the telephone or computer of a target of surveillance, while "trap and trace devices" record the number of any incoming call to a targeted phone number. The Justice Department has classified its use of this section. This provision sunsets in 2005.

Section 216, entitled "Modification of Authorities Relating to Use of Pen Registers and Trap and Trace Devices," requires courts to order "the installation and use of a pen register or trap and trace device anywhere within the United States," if the government asserts that it is "relevant to an ongoing criminal investigation." The vocabulary of this section is important, as always. The phrase "relevant to" means, of course, that such an investigation is not necessarily "directly of" a crime or criminal. Further, the use of "criminal investigation" expands the scope of the Act to include use of such tools to investigate crimes of all stripes, not just those related to terrorism. Section 216 requires courts to order tracking devices for both telephone and internet "dialing, routing, addressing and signaling information and content," relevant to any *criminal* investigation (i.e., not limited to terrorism investigations). This section does require the government to keep a record of who they spy on in this way, but they are not required to present it to any court until thirty days after they officially close the investigation. Additionally, this section does have a vaguely worded provision stating that "wiretaps may not intercept the content" of emails, only addresses and subject headings. Under Section 216, internet service providers are shielded from prosecution for allowing governmental eavesdropping on their clients. It is under this section that PATRIOT is said to allow the FBI to use the program called "Carnivore," which literally "eats up" all information coming through an ISP, storing it in a government data bank, with files created for the ISP users.[11] These files will contain content information as well as web sites visited and persons emailed. Section 216 has no sunset clause.

In conjunction with Section 216, Section 225 provides legal protection of those government agents who tap into phone and email systems in order to extract information on people. Now, should a person become aware that any given communication company s/he uses has provided the government content of their communications, that person has no legal recourse against the company providing such information.

Section 218, "Foreign Intelligence Information," relaxes the standards that were previously the law. FISA set standards that required that such governmental spying be restricted to the gathering of foreign intelligence. Now, under Section 218, such intelligence represents only one "significant purpose" of such actions (i.e. not the primary purpose), which can now be justified by any criminal investigation. All that is required is that the Attorney General state that such a search is needed for "an ongoing intelligence investigation."[12] The FISA court approved 934 such warrants in 2001; 1,228 in 2002 (the number was consistently below 900 in the 1990's).[13] This section sunsets in 2005.

Title III: "International Money Laundering Abatement and Anti-Terrorist Financing Act of 2001"

This Title concerns economic matters, such as banking and international money laundering. This is the lengthiest section of the Patriot Act, and in essence simply permits the government to have access to all banking and financial records of individuals they are investigating, without the knowledge or permission of said individuals, for any criminal or intelligence activities the government wishes to perform. Specifically, Section 314 requires brokers and dealers to report "suspicious activity." No one contacted by the government for such information may report it to the person being investigated (Section 351).

This Title applies to "financial institutions," not persons, and thus does not fit the purpose for our examination of the act here. Moreover, the vast majority of persons doing banking will not be affected by this Title. As C. William Michaels rightfully explains it, for a "private banking account" to come under these particular requirements, it must have minimum aggregate deposits of $1 million, be established on behalf of one or more persons having a beneficial ownership in the account, and be managed by an officer or agent of a bank acting as a "liaison" for the account's "direct or beneficial owner."[14]

However, if one were a *relative* of a person who fits this kind of banking activity, that relative opening a private account would be susceptible to the new and expanded rules of information gathering allowed under this Title. It is also noteworthy that Title III does not require a court order for investigators to gather massive amounts of financial information on persons who do such banking; nor are those investigators required to show any kind of probable cause for their activities of financial surveillance. Section 314 permits government surveillance of the economic activities of nonprofit organizations that might be involved in money laundering, even if they are involved in such activities unknowingly. This Section also protects those banking institutions that report their customers from lawsuits by those person or persons being reported on.

Sections 316-320 widen the government's power to seize assets from those who are in any way connected with any financing of terrorism. Of special interest is Section 319, "Forfeiture of Funds in United States Interbank Accounts," which allows a federal investigator to obtain any information from any bank account simply by "requesting" it. The institution being so "asked" then has 120 hours to supply all of this information to the federal agent. It is not specifically stated in this section that the account must have a foreign connection.

Section 326 requires the Treasury Department to provide new minimal standards for identifying new bank customers. It does not specify what type of identification will be required in the future, but whatever regulations are put into place, they will apply to all persons who attempt to open new bank accounts, including all U.S. citizens.

Section 358 permits the government to collect the credit reports of U.S. persons, simply on the written notification that such a report is necessary for an investigation. No court order is required for the feds to obtain this credit information on U.S. persons.

Title III may only be "sunset" by an act of Congress in 2005. Otherwise, this Title is to become permanent U.S. law. Although Title III is by far the longest Title of the PATRIOT Act, given the extremely limited applicability of this Title, both in terms of rights and to persons, we would be well served by moving to the next Title of the PATRIOT Act.

Title IV: "Protecting the Border"

This Title has a number of provisions in it, all of them dealing with immigrants and/or foreign nationals. This Title is incredible for the vastly expanded powers it gives to the federal government to arrest and detain aliens. Perhaps equally disturbing, none of the sections of Title IV has a sunset clause; the Title is now permanent U.S. law.

For civil rights advocates, the most problematic section is 411, "Enhanced Immigration Provisions." This section does several things. First of all, it defines "domestic terrorism" as "acts dangerous to human life that are a violation of the criminal laws . . . [and] that appear to be intended...to influence the policy of government by intimidation or coercion." Second, it expands the requirement of who can be exported under the blanket of being defined as a terrorist. Now, any immigrant who commits a crime using a "weapon or dangerous device" may be deported as a "terrorist." Third, Section 411 allows for removal of a non-citizen for providing support to an organization not designated as "terrorist" prior to the passing of the Patriot Act. Fourth, it expands the definition of what it means to "engage in a terrorist activity" to one that includes "soliciting funds or other things of value," for any "political, social, or other similar group" that the Secretary of State brands either as a "terrorist organization" or an organization that the Secretary holds "undermines U.S. efforts to reduce or eliminate terrorist activities." In conjunction with this, a "terrorist organization" is now to be defined as "two or more individuals, whether organized or not," which engages in activities supporting terrorism. What constitutes "support" of "terrorism" is not defined. However, what is clear is that, for example, an immigrant who collects money for a charity that comes to be targeted by the government as a "terrorist" organization, and who thus gets arrested for supporting a terrorist organization, will now have to "demonstrate that he did not know, and should not reasonably have known, that the solicitation would further the organization's terrorist activity," in the words of Section 411.

But this is not all. Section 411 also adds the following pieces of legislation. First it legislates that no immigrant who belongs to a group "whose public endorsement of acts of terrorist activity the Secretary of State has determined undermines United States efforts to reduce or eliminate terrorist activities" will be allowed into the U.S. Second, no spouse or child of any person suspected by the government of being "in association with terrorist organizations" or in any way "supporting terrorism," will be permitted entry into the U.S. No definition of "association with terrorist organizations" is given. Finally, "[No] alien who the Secretary of State . . . determines has been associated with a terrorist organization and intends while in the United States to engage solely, principally, or *incidentally* in activities that could endanger the welfare, safety, or security of the United States" will be admitted. (emphasis mine)

Another point at issue in Section 411 concerns the retroactive application of the deportation of citizens for the activities described above. Thus, a person who gave a donation to an organization s/he presumed to be a charitable one, but later is designated a "terrorist organization" by the U.S. government, is liable to prosecution with the retroactive clause of 411.

A further issue in Section 411, pointed out by David Cole, is the double standard concerning what constitutes "terrorist activity" between U.S. citizens and immigrant non-citizens.[15] We have seen the definition of "domestic terrorism," but as Cole points out, "terrorist activity" is defined in a much broader fashion as it applies to immigrants, to include support of the otherwise lawful and nonviolent activities of virtually any group that has used violence, and any use or threat to use a weapon against person or property ('other than for mere personal monetary gain').[16]

Thus for a non-citizen, "terrorism" includes "wholly nonviolent activity and ordinary crimes of violence."[17]

Section 412, "Mandatory Detention of Suspected Terrorists; Habeas Corpus; Judicial Review," expands the power of the U.S. government regarding detention and expulsion of immigrants from the U.S. Specifically, it states that the Attorney General need have only "reasonable grounds" to believe that an immigrant poses a threat to national security, and on these grounds alone he may detain that immigrant for up to seven days, unless "removal is unlikely in the foreseeable future, [in the event of which they] may be detained for additional periods of up to six months." These "reasonable grounds" include a judgment by the Attorney General that an immigrant has engaged in "any...activity that endangers the national security of the United States." When such a person has been arrested, s/he will now not be released until the Attorney General can either deport him/her, or state that s/he is no longer involved in terrorist activities. By the ruling of this section, the only court review permitted for such actions on the part of the government is a habeas corpus review. This is the section under which the Justice Department has rounded up over a thousand immigrants to the U.S., without charging them with a crime.

Furthermore, regarding deportation, if the immigrant is to be deported, but the deportation is "unlikely in the foreseeable future," the Justice Department may keep him/her detained for up to an additional six months. Also, the Attorney General may now detain immigrants solely on his word that he has "reasonable grounds to believe" that such a person is engaged in terrorist activities.[18]

Section 413, "Multilateral Cooperation Against Terrorists," echoes a prominent and consistent theme in PATRIOT, and that is permission for information sharing between government agencies. However, in this case, it is far more reaching than simple information sharing between various departments of our own government. In this case, the Justice Department is permitted to share its information on aliens with foreign governments.

Section 414, entitled "Visa Integrity and Security," allows the Justice Department to use a system PATRIOT refers to as the "Integrated Entry and Exit Data System." This system allows the Department to track arrival and departure of immigrants. It was mandated to be ready for use at airports and seaports by December 31, 2003. Combine this with Section 416, "Foreign Student Monitoring Program," which allows the Justice Department to monitor the geographical location of all foreign citizens in the country and one can see that the intent here is obviously to keep close watch on every aspect of the movements of an immigrant while s/he is in the U.S., with very broad authority for arrest and deportation of immigrants should they "step out of line."

Title V: "Removing Obstacles to Investigating Terrorism"

This Title allows the U.S. government to conduct wide-ranging and deep information gathering on citizens and non-citizens alike. Specifically, Section 501 permits the Department of Justice to present rewards to those persons who help them "combat terrorism and defend the Nation against terrorist acts." These rewards can be up to $250,000.

Section 503, "DNA Identification of Terrorists and Other Violent Offenders," vastly expands the crimes for which DNA samples will be taken. Now, "any crime of violence" or "any attempt or conspiracy to commit" violent or terrorist crimes will be used as a pretext to collect DNA samples from the convicted person.

Section 504 allows more information sharing, both electronic and physical, between government departments for purposes of investigation of potential "grave hostile acts of a foreign power or an agent of a foreign power" (i.e. not just immigrants or foreign nationals, but also U.S. citizens, if they can be described by the Justice Department as so acting for another "power").

Section 505 is an important one. It is called "Miscellaneous National Security Authorities," and it allows the FBI access to an extensive amount of private information about U.S. persons (again, citizens included in this). Thus, the application of this section is not restricted to immigrants. It allows information to be collected on a person from telephone records, financial records, and consumer reports. Here an investigating agent of the FBI is permitted to require persons and institutions to produce personal records of a target of surveillance, even if that target is not suspected of espionage or criminal activity. All that is required is a "national security letter," which can be issued by any field office of the FBI, rather than by the Justice Department supervisors.[19] This letter need only state that the information is needed for an "international terrorism" investigation. Furthermore, there is no court order required for such actions, nor is judicial review permitted for such activities under this section. In addition, a gag order is placed on those who are required to turn information over the government. The only limit to such information gathering is activities that are protected by the First Amendment. According to http://slate.msn.com, in a 2003 ACLU suit over this section, the FBI was required to produce documentation concerning how it had used this section. It produced over five pages of logs of persons contacted in this fashion.[20] In addition to this, Section 506 extends the authority of the U.S. Secret Service, so that they may conduct as wide-ranging an investigation as the FBI.

Section 507 allows the government to order colleges "to disclose complete educational records of any individual under investigation." It also permits the government to "retain, disseminate, and use such records." Section 508 allows "the Attorney General (or his designee) to collect reports, records, and information (including individually identifiable information)," and to "retain, disseminate and use . . . such information, consistent with such guidelines as the Attorney General shall issue." In other words, the government can collect whatever information on whatever people they want, for whatever purposes they want to collect such information, spread it around among themselves, and never tell anyone, least of all the person who is being researched, that they have collected such information on them. This type of activity is sanctioned throughout the PATRIOT Act, but is specifically laid out here.

Title VI: "Providing for Victims of Terrorism, Public Safety Officers, and Their Families"

This is one of the least controversial Titles of the PATRIOT Act, expanding the use of money to provide for the families of terrorist attacks.

Title VII: "Increased Information Sharing for Critical Infrastructure Protection"

This Title once again expands information sharing between federal agencies and state and local law enforcement agencies. This is the last remaining wall preventing a complete network of information on U.S. persons available to every level of law enforcement in this country.

Title VIII: "Strengthening the Criminal Laws against Terrorism"

This Title extends the governmental power to spy on citizens on a permanent basis, as there is no sunset provision for any of the sections of this Title. This Title is also open to application to U.S. citizens, as it does not specifically designate use with aliens only.

Section 802 of this Title defines "Domestic Terrorism" in this very broad way: "acts dangerous to human life that are a violation of the criminal laws" if "they appear to be intended . . . to influence the policy of a government by intimidation or coercion," and if "they occur primarily within the territorial jurisdiction of the United States." Note that this definition includes *any* crime, not just that of terrorism.

Section 808 creates a new "federal crime of terrorism." It is an all-inclusive list of activities will legitimate a federal government investigation. The "laundry list" of crimes here is very long, but it is well worth quoting it in full. From now on, the following crimes are to be classified as "terrorist:"

> Destruction of aircraft or aircraft facilities, violence at international airports, arson within special maritime and territorial jurisdiction, [use of] biological or chemical weapons, congressional, cabinet, and Supreme Court assassination or kidnapping, [use of] nuclear materials or plastic explosives, arson and bombing of Government property risking or causing death, arson and bombing of property used in interstate commerce, relating to killing or attempted killing during an attack on a Federal facility with a dangerous weapon, conspiracy to murder, kidnap, or maim persons abroad, [crimes related to] computers, killing or attempting to kill officers and employees of the United States, murder

or manslaughter of foreign officials, official guests, or internationally protected persons, hostage taking, destruction of communication lines, stations, or systems, injury to buildings or property within special maritime and territorial jurisdiction of the United States, destruction of an energy facility, Presidential and Presidential staff assassination and kidnapping, wrecking trains, terrorist attacks and other acts of violence against mass transportation systems, destruction of national defense materials, premises, or utilities, violence against maritime navigation, violence against maritime fixed platforms, certain homicides and other violence against United States nationals occurring outside of the United States, use of weapons of mass destruction, acts of terrorism transcending national boundaries, harboring terrorists, providing material support to terrorists, providing material support to terrorist organizations, torture, sabotage of nuclear facilities or fuel, aircraft piracy, assault on a flight crew with a dangerous weapon, [use of] explosive or incendiary devices, or endangerment of human life by means of weapons, on aircraft, destruction of interstate gas or hazardous liquid pipeline facility.

This would seem to be the decisive definition of "terrorism" provided by the USA PATRIOT Act. Although this is not clearly stated in PATRIOT, it would seem that all other Titles and Sections would be measured in their application by this expansive definition.

Section 809 lifts all statute of limitations on any alleged "terrorist offense" that "resulted in, or created a foreseeable risk of death or serious bodily injury to another person." This retroactively applies to all such acts committed even before the passage of the PATRIOT Act.

Sections 810 and 811 provide the penalties for the "terrorist" acts listed in 808. These generally begin with 10-20 year sentences, up to life in prison, should a death occur while such acts were engaged in.

Title IX: "Improved Intelligence"

Section 901, again, permits information sharing of information collected on U.S. persons by the federal government. This time the information sharing permitted is between the Justice Department and the CIA.

Section 903, "Sense of Congress on the Establishment and Maintenance of Intelligence Relationships to Acquire Information on Terrorists and Terrorist Activities," exhorts every member of the intelligence community on the federal level to

make every effort to establish and maintain intelligence relationships with any person, entity, or group for the purpose
of engaging in lawful intelligence activities, including the
acquisition of information on the identity, location, fi-
nances, affiliations, capabilities, plans, or intentions of a
terrorist or terrorist organization.

In other words, the encouragement of this section is for all
government employees to spy on others. This could well include the
neighbor or even friend of such an employee.

Title X: "Miscellaneous"

Seemingly aware of the potential for Justice Department abuse
of the powers granted to it under PATRIOT, Section 1001, "Review of
the Department of Justice," requires the Department to "designate one
official who shall review information and receive complaints alleging
abuses of civil rights and civil liberties by employees and officials of
the Department of Justice."

Section 1005, "First Responders Assistance Act," allocates
$25 million per grant to local law enforcement officials to do such
things as "purchase technology and equipment for intelligence gathering and analysis functions, including wiretap, pen links, cameras, and
computer hardware and software." These funds are also for "intelligence gathering and analysis techniques." Remember that these large
grants are for information gathering, "including the formation of full-
time intelligence gathering and analysis units," at the local level.

Sections 1008 and 1009 direct feasibility studies between the
Justice Department, State Department, and Transportation Department.
The study under Section 1008 concerns the use of a biometric (i.e. fingerprint) identifier scanning system as part of the customs process. The
study under Section 1009 concerns the potential use by airlines of the
names of passengers who are suspected of terrorist activities, as defined
in the very broad way by PATRIOT.

It is important to note, in conclusion, that not every Title and
section in USA PATRIOT is a threat to civil rights. Title VI, "Providing for Victims of Terrorism, Public Safety Officers, and Their Families" demonstrates a very healthy commitment on the part of the Federal government to aid families who are the victims of terrorist attacks.
But as innocuous as this title and other sections can be, they are too few
and far between to give PATRIOT a "thumbs up" concerning the protection of our rights as U.S. persons.

Now that we have reviewed the main documents at issue and asked some questions concerning their constitutional legitimacy, we are in a position to engage in some analysis of the USA PATRIOT Act. This will be the purpose of the next chapter.

Notes

1 Common Dreams, 9/8/03.

2 The term "terrorism" is never defined in this legislation. This lack of definition essentially allows the Justice Department to define a "terrorist" in any way it wants, and apply its newly wrought powers to such a person.

3 For more detail on this, see Nat Hentoff, "Terrorizing the Bill of Rights," *Village Voice*, November 20, 2001. See also Hentoff, *The War on the Bill of Rights and the Gathering Resistance* (New York: Seven Stories Press, 2003).

4 Diane Rehm Show, WAMU, 8/20/03. Stated by Laura Murphy, Director of ACLU Washington Legislative Office.

5 Chang, Nancy, ""How Democracy Dies: The War on Our Civil Liberties," in *Lost Liberties: Ashcroft and the Assault on Personal Freedom* (New York: The New Press, 2003), p. 36.

6 See Michael, C. William, *No Greater Threat: America After September 11 and the Rise of the National Security State* (New York: Algora Publishing, 2002), p. 44.

7 Ibid, p. 47.

8 http://slate.msn.com

9 ibid.

10 See http://slate.msn.com, "A Guide to the Patriot Act," 9/10/2003; Dahlia Lithwick and Julia Turner.

11 Nancy Chang, www.ccr-ny.org. "The USA PATRIOT Act: What's So Patriotic About Trampling on the Bill of Rights?"

12 For more on this, see ibid.

13 http://slate.msn.com

14 Michaels, op. cit., pages 78-79.

15 Ibid, p. 58.

16 Ibid.

17 Ibid.

18 See Chang, "The USA PATRIOT Act," op. cit.

19 http://slate.msn.com, op.cit.

20 http://slate.msn.com, op.cit.

Chapter Three: Does the PATRIOT Act Trample Civil Liberties?

What conclusions can we draw when we compare the philosophy of John Locke, and the Bill of Rights, to the USA Patriot Act?

At the very least, we are warranted in concluding that the USA PATRIOT Act goes far beyond the traditional view of human rights and jurisprudence. That, presumably, even Mr. Ashcroft would admit. But what the PATRIOT Act really does is to take the expanded power given to the government to spy on foreign countries, agents, and terrorists, and shifts it into their ability to spy on American citizens. When it makes this move, it butts squarely against both the Bill of Rights and the traditional practice of American jurisprudence; for example, the idea that U.S. persons are to be considered innocent until they are proven guilty in a court of law. This chapter proposes to look at the conflicts between PATRIOT and American civil rights, specifically with regard to the Bill of Rights. The argument here will be that the USA PATRIOT Act, and the Domestic Security Enhancement Act of 2003 (DSEA), both violate in substantial ways both the spirit (philosophy) and the letter of the U.S. Constitution.

I. The "Spirit of the Law" as Found in the Philosophy of Rights Underpinning the United States Constitution

A cursory examination of the legal traditions precedent to the U.S. Constitution indicates clearly that neither the USA PATRIOT Act nor the DSEA upholds the tradition of respecting the rights of the people to due process, probable cause, habeas corpus, excessive bail, or cruel and unusual punishment. We will examine the specifics of this assertion below. For now, we begin our analysis of the two pieces of legislation outlined in this text with the philosophy that was the capstone defense of the legal practices that became part of the Declaration of Independence and the U.S. Constitution: John Locke and his philosophy of natural rights. Although the natural rights tradition is not widely held today, we can still defend rights-based thinking philosophically by holding that such rights have been agreed to by the members of a society and codified as a result of this agreement. In such a defense, we can bypass the problem of asserting them to be "natural" rights. One way or another, it is undeniable that the rights Locke defended are the cornerstone to the form of democracy that has existed in the United States from its inception until now.

The concept of rights maintained by Locke is very general in comparison to the details of the procedures for fighting a war on terrorism. There is obviously, then, some room for interpretation. On the other hand, there are some philosophical principles in Locke that seem to argue decisively against the actions of the government regarding its people as seen in both PATRIOT Acts I and II. For example, when Locke declares that the law of nature is our reason, which means that we each have the ability to determine our own actions without being compelled to act by the force of another or others, it would be difficult, at best, to square this conception of reason with a carte blanche for governmental spying and deportation of its citizens and/or foreign nationals (PATRIOT, Section 322). Nor would he likely be in agreement with the provision of PATRIOT which compels citizens not to "attempt to influence governmental policy by intimidation or coercion" (Section 802). Even less would he agree with the idea that a citizen could lose their citizenship for vague and imprecise reasons, not including their expressed intent to renounce it (DSEA, Section 501).

Furthermore, the first law that reason generates instructs us to engage in mutual preservation of lives, liberties, and possessions, such that "the end of law is not to abolish or restrain, but to preserve and enlarge freedom."[1] Further, this law of nature, reason, is that which founds the right of the people to pursue our own "innocent ends," without interference from government. When that freedom is severely truncated, as we see in the PATRIOT Acts I and II, then one is justified in concluding that PATRIOT does not defend the right to freedom of which Locke speaks. One can make the case that such freedom is precisely what is limited in PATRIOT, Section 411, which limits what activities may be innocently engaged in by immigrants. See also DSEA, Sections 102 (where one who gathers information on the government is to be deemed "a foreign agent," instead of a "citizen"), 125 and 126 (permitting government gathering credit reports and economic data on citizens), 201 and 202 (suspensions of the Freedom of Information Act), and 404, for other examples of the types of liberties that Locke would undoubtedly find disturbing from a natural rights perspective.

The other side to this argument suggests that the law of reason is also a law which instructs us to preserve "all of humanity," not just ourselves. Where there is a threat to the society, Locke is clear that this person or persons must be "destroyed . . . as any other wild beast."[2] Supporters of the PATRIOT Act argue that this is what the Act attempts to do. However, what is being preserved by such an Act as

PATRIOT? It is telling that the Assistant Attorney General, Daniel J. Bryant, spelled out the intention of PATRIOT:

> As commander-in-chief, the President must be able to use whatever means necessary to prevent attacks upon the United States . . . Here, for Fourth Amendment purposes, the right to self-defense is not that of an individual, but that of the nation and its citizens . . . If the government's heightened interest in self-defense justifies the use of deadly force, then it certainly would also justify warrantless searches.[3]

How might Locke respond to such an assertion? Given that the entire purpose of the government is to protect the citizens who consent to its existence and power, and given Locke's complete disdain for absolute and arbitrary governmental power over citizens,[4] we can be fairly certain that he would not countenance such an assertion by the Assistant Attorney General. What the latter is attempting to do is to take the natural right to self-preservation and apply it to the State, whereas Locke would have it distinctly applied to individuals. Specifically, Locke states that

> there is danger still, that they [the Legislative is always in power] will think themselves to have a distinct interest, from the rest of the Community; and so will apt to increase their own riches and power, by taking, what they think fit, from the People. For a Man's Property is not at all secure . . . if he who commands those Subjects, have Power to take from any private Man, what part he pleases of his Property, and use and dispose of it as he thinks good.[5]

But for Locke, the freedom of the people trumps any right of government. As we have seen, "he would take away my freedom declares war on me . . . This freedom from Absolute, Arbitrary Power," is so necessary to self-preservation that one cannot forfeit it without simultaneously forfeiting "his Preservation and Life altogether."[6] Although Locke held these rights to exist in the state of nature, they transfer over to the political order when the social compact exists, since the origin and continued existence of the government depends on the consent of the governed, not the other way around.[7] It would be hard to argue that legislative acts which put so much power into one branch of government follow Locke's proscribing this from happening. For example, see PATRIOT, Section 411 and 802 (described immediately above), and DSEA Sections 106 (shielding illegal federal wiretappers from citizen prosecution); 109 (secret court with great powers); 123 (amending judicial supervision of Department of Justice activities[8]); 128 (Justice Department can write its own subpoenas, without court order or supervision); 204 (requires court approval of Justice Department requests to submit ex parte evidence); 322 (extradition of immigrants for crimes or unapproved political activities); 506 (allows Attorney General to determine place of deportation, with or without treaty with U.S. Senate).

Again, the "property" that each of us possesses in our "lives, liberties, and estates" is such that, without our consent, it may not be taken away. Thus, the government may not seize property without the person consenting to it (assuming, of course, that such property is not being used to commit a crime—i.e. is being used for "innocent ends," in the words of Locke), for the preservation of such property is the raison d'etre of the government to begin with. This makes "sneak and peak" and rights of seizure granted in PATRIOT (Section 213) immoral according to the Lockean doctrine. In addition, see Section 506 (explained immediately above), and DSEA, Section 105 (allows information gathering by the Justice Department, whether of a criminal nature or not).

Another counterargument might be that according to Locke, the rights of self-preservation and the punishment of wrongdoers are surrendered to the government, and that the function of the government is to preserve the common good. Furthermore, Locke acknowledges that the government "decides all the differences that may happen . . . and punishes those Offenses which any Member hath committed against Society, with such Penalties as the Law has established." Such Acts as PATRIOT are intended to insure that preservation and common good by rooting out the wrongdoers for punishment. Locke permits all this.

Once again, however, this would be an incomplete reading of Locke, since he is quite clear that the authority of government has its limits, even in the face of the common good. Governmental authority cannot be absolute or arbitrary over its people, for "no Body can transfer to another more power than he has in himself."[9] Locke extends a maximal degree of freedom to the individual, on the grounds that no one person has absolute or arbitrary power over his or her own life, liberty, or possessions. The only power that can be given and taken is that which can preserve these rights to a maximal degree. Therefore, the government has no power to "destroy, enslave, or designedly to impoverish the Subjects."[10] This limit is spelled out clearly when Locke states explicitly that the government cannot take any of a person's property without his/her consent. Even more to the point, "it is a mistake to think, that the Supream or Legislative Power of any Commonwealth, can do what it will, and dispose of the Estates of the Subject arbitrarily, or take any part of them at pleasure."[11]

Thus, for Locke, there is a maximal amount of freedom the individual has, even in civil society, provided his actions stay within the bounds of the natural law (i.e. self-preservation and the preservation of all. For ways the PATRIOT Act and DSEA do not fulfill this, see PATRIOT, Section 215; 412; take your pick of a DSEA Section 1). This maximal amount of freedom, which government is instituted to protect, is what Locke refers to as "the freedom to our own person."[12] As we saw in Chapter One, such a right is virtually absolute in Locke's thinking.

In conclusion, we can see that the USA PATRIOT Act and the Domestic Security Enhancement Act of 2003 fall short of preserving the spirit or philosophy of the Bill of Rights. Now let us examine the letter of the law in the Bill of Rights itself, to see if the PATRIOT Acts I and II uphold our cherished democratic tradition in the United States.

Before beginning this examination, however, it is important to note some things that will be repeated as our analysis progresses. First of all, we would do well to keep in mind the general principle of liberty as it is defined and highlighted by Locke. We will see this principle at work in the Bill of Rights. Second, prime among those rights is the freedom of speech. That is why it is the *first* Amendment to the Constitution. Third, from a strictly constitutional view, the First, Fourth, and Fifth Amendments are said to directly apply to "the people," not specifically the citizens. The Supreme Court has consistently taken note of that, and has consistently ruled that these rights apply to all persons on American soil, not just citizens.[13]

II. Probable Cause (the Fourth Amendment)

"Probable cause" means that the government must have "reasonable grounds" for conducting searches and surveillances on U.S. persons. While in some cases this requirement is lifted by the courts (usually on a case-by-case basis), it is still the guiding principle in the jurisprudence of rights cases.

How does PATRIOT perhaps ignore or override this esteemed practice in American law enforcement? We may list them straightaway:

A. The continual switch of terminology in PATRIOT from the FISA requirement for "evidence" to the PATRIOT allowance for "suspicion" only, is a direct contravention of the Fourth Amendment requirement for probable cause. Even more importantly, if "suspicion" is all that is now required for a search or seizure, then the judicial system has been effectively bypassed, in favor of Justice Department interests.

B. Section 214—No warrant is required for use of trap and trace devices; just "relevance to an ongoing terrorist investigation."

C. Section 215—The FBI does not need to suspect the person of wrongdoing in order to seize evidence. In addition, delayed notification of warrant is permitted. This section also repeals a restriction on governmental seizure of information. FISA had required "specific and articulable facts giving reason to believe that the person to whom the records pertain is a foreign power or an agent of a foreign power." It also repeals a restriction on what records were allowed to be seized, placing no limit on which "tangible thing" may be gathered up by government agents.[14]

D. Section 216—This section allows vast government absorbing of information, under three different rubrics that apply to probable cause. The first concerns a government software program called "Carnivore," which literally "eats up" an entire ISP's email. It has been argued that this section opens up government use of that program to any target of intelligence gathering. More importantly, this provision is not only permanent, but "paves the way for a new era of national-level electronic surveillance and investigation by federal agencies, not necessarily restricted to terrorism, less susceptible to challenge, and not subject to extensive court supervision or review."[15]

E. Section 218—FISA allowed probable cause exceptions when wiretapping foreign agents when the "primary purpose" was for intelligence gathering. PATRIOT suspends probable cause altogether in favor of wiretapping for "significant purpose" involving *criminal* (i.e. not limited to terrorist) investigations.

F. Section 412—No hearing, nor evidence presentation is required for jailing immigrants under this Section. This applies to *suspected*, not proved, terrorists. Perhaps most decisively, this type of detention is only constitutional where there is a risk of the person fleeing or of danger to society.[16]

Again, the main Constitutional issue here is the Fourth Amendment requirement that "probable cause" is required to engage in such actions. The Supreme Court has already ruled that such Constitutional protection applies to both citizens and immigrants.[17]

G. Section 505—This Section forces anyone who holds information on a target of investigation to turn over the information they have, even if they are not suspected of espionage or of criminal activity. Further, all that is required for information seizure is a "letter of national security" which may be written by any FBI field agent, not the upper management of the Department of Justice.

How does "Patriot II" (DSEA) violate probable cause?

A. Section 101 eliminates the requirement of probable cause for eavesdropping on individual U.S. persons, and replaces it with "suspicion."

B. Section 124, in contradiction to the Fourth Amendment, would allow for the government to eavesdrop on any function of an electronic device without specifying the probable cause for the action. Critics submit that using a cell phone to transmit illegal information does not entail that one will use one's email functions of that cell phone to do likewise. The Fourth Amendment requires what is called "specificity" with regard to such eavesdropping.[18]

III. Privacy

The main issue in PATRIOT, Titles V and VIII, is the right to privacy. This may come as a surprise to many, but prior to 1890, Americans had little but notion of "privacy rights." It is certainly not a right directly contained in the Constitution. However, since 1890, it has been a right that the U.S. Supreme Court has declared to be "self-evident" and constitutionally implied. Specifically, in Olmstead v. U.S., in 1928, Justice Brandeis, writing for the majority, made the following claim:

> The right to be left alone—the most comprehensive of our rights, and the right most valued by civilized men. To protect that right, every unjustifiable intrusion by the government upon the privacy of the individual, whatever the means employed, must be deemed a violation of the Fourth Amendment.[19]

This is the right that the Supreme Court appealed to in Griswold v. Connecticut, regarding the right to the use of artificial contraception by marriage partners, and again in Roe v. Wade, concerning the right of a woman to procure an abortion. The right to privacy has become a well-marked and Court-supported interpretation of the Fourth Amendment to the U.S. Constitution.

With this in mind, we may highlight some of the sections where PATRIOT oversteps its bounds with regard to privacy rights guaranteed by the Bill of Rights.

A. Section 203 allows government agencies who do investigation on any criminal matter to share that information with other agencies. This will be discussed in more detail in Section VII, "Other Rights Issues Raised by PATRIOT and "Patriot II"," below.

B. Section 206 allows "roving wiretaps." Thus, if the FBI is investigating someone who uses a library computer, *any* person who also uses that computer can be monitored by the FBI without their knowledge or consent.

C. Section 213 permits "sneak-and-peek" searches that violate the Fourth Amendment and also Rule 41(d) of the Federal Rules of Criminal Procedure. The FRCP requires that "the officer taking property under the warrant shall give to the person from whom or from whose premises the property was taken a copy of the warrant and a receipt for the property taken or shall leave the copy and receipt at the place from which the property was taken."[20]

Further, this Section allows delayed notification of search warrant prohibits the person searched from monitoring what was searched or what was taken. Said person also is barred from knowing where the property was taken.

D. Section 214 allows pen registers and trap and trace devices

E. Section 215 allows the FBI to require any record of any person from anyone, and requires judges to approve of it. There is no requirement for the government to provide specific facts supporting that a person is an agent of a foreign power, as required by FISA.[21]

F. Section 216 permits tracking devices for telephone and internet dialing, routing addressing and signaling information. While the government is forbidden from routinely capturing the actual content of email messages, this Section goes beyond what has been the norm by allowing the subject line of emails and any web sites visited to be monitored.

G. Section 218 allows the collection and sharing of intelligence information by law enforcement communities for intelligence gathering only, not for criminal activity. This changes the legal tradition radically, in that criminal law enforcement, once separated from foreign intelligence gathering, is no more. This also breaks down any separation between law enforcement and intelligence gatherers by allowing cooperation between the two.

Significantly, the "primary purpose" of espionage intelligence gathering under FISA becomes "significant purpose" for *criminal* investigation in PATRIOT.

How does "Patriot II" (DSEA) violate privacy?

Section 104 allows surveillance of spoken communication of U.S. persons, without court order, on any electronic device owned by a foreign government.

Section 126 allows the government to obtain financial records of individuals, such as credit reports, without that person's knowledge or consent, without court order, and without judicial review.

Section 128 allows administrative subpoenas, not court order or judicial oversight of record collecting of individuals.

Section 303 has as its main issue what is included under the right to privacy. A DNA sample includes quite a bit more information than does a simple fingerprint. The latter can only be used for identification purposes, while the former contains inherited and other proclivities for diseases, for parental lineage, and for the genetic history of the family of the individual. Thus, the possibilities for abuse are numerous, and such a practice, as a result, requires very careful monitoring. However, no monitoring at all is called for by this section of the act.

Section 311 allows information sharing between all federal investigative agencies, as well as between federal, state, and local law enforcement. There is no limitation to information required for a criminal investigation; it is simply "to assist the official receiving that information in the performance of the official duties of that official."

IV. Checks and Balances

Checks and balances between the Judicial, Executive, and Legislative branches of government provide a guarantee that governmental power will not be consolidated or abused by one branch. The threats to this fundamental structure of constitutional democracy in the U.S. may be seen in the following sections of PATRIOT.

A. Section 203—Allows information sharing between the FBI, CIA, INS, and other federal agencies without judicial oversight. It also permits disclosure of grand jury information without judicial supervision. This applies to all *criminal* (not just terrorist) investigations, and includes all U.S. persons (i.e. citizens and non-citizens alike).

B. Section 206—no judicial review permitted of roving wiretaps.

C. Section 214—Requires a judge to give a court order for pen registers and trap and trace devices.

D. Section 215—Requires a judge to court order seizures of "any tangible thing" they request, merely by claiming that it is "sought for" a terrorism investigation OR that it is for "clandestine intelligence activities."

E. Section 216—Requires the judge to issue a court order for pen registers and trap and trace devices. It also permits *no* judicial supervision of activities under this section.

F. Section 412—No hearings required before jailing aliens/immigrants.

G. Section 505—No judicial review permitted of the activities of forcing people to turn over information on other people.

How does "Patriot II" violate checks and balances?

A. Section 103—eliminates court orders for and judicial review of surveillance for 15 days after an attack on the U.S. has been declared by the President.

B. Section 104—allows surveillance of spoken communication of U.S. persons, without court order, on any electronic device owned by a foreign government.

C. Section 106 creates a shield against prosecution for wiretappers acting without court order.

D. Section 126—Allows the government to obtain financial records of individuals, such as credit reports, without that person's knowledge or consent, without court order, and without judicial review.

E. Section 128—Allows administrative subpoenas, not court order or judicial oversight of record collecting of individuals.

F. Section 321—Citizens of the U.S. could be deported to a country, even where no treaty exists between the U.S. government and the foreign government of destination.

G. Section 322—Courts are stripped of the authority to review extradition requests.

H. Section 504—rescinds habeas corpus rights of immigrants.

It is important to note, in concluding this section, that the way Mr. Ashcroft has gotten around the need for judicial or Congressional oversight has been to classify information or simply to refuse to answer inquiries from Congress.

V. Due Process (the Fifth Amendment)

Guaranteed by the Fifth Amendment, this clause requires the government to follow established rules (not specifically mentioned in the Bill of Rights), and not act arbitrarily. This includes the right to be presumed innocent until proven guilty, and the right to have the state prove its case beyond a reasonable doubt.[22]

Under PATRIOT, there are a host of due process issues.

A. Section 411 presents a new definition of "terrorist" ("where two or more are gathered"), plus the definition of "engaging in terrorist activity" ("providing material support for terrorist organizations"). In so doing, it allows prosecution through "Guilt by association," a direct undermining of the First Amendment. The Supreme Court has ruled that "Guilt by association is alien to the traditions of a free society and to the First Amendment itself."[23] Also, the Supreme Court regularly struck down laws that penalized association with the Communist Party, absent proof that the individual actually intended to further the party's ends.[24]

Georgetown law professor David Cole argues succinctly that "citizens have a constitutional right to endorse terrorist organizations or terrorist activity, so long as their speech is not intended and likely to produce imminent lawless action."[25] More importantly, keeping people out of the country simply because they hold political views not amicable to the reigning ones in a given U.S. administration directly contravenes the principles of liberty and freedom of speech that we adhere to, both in spirit and in law.

It bears repeating that the First, Fourth, and Fifth Amendments have been ruled by the Supreme Court to directly to apply to "the people," not specifically the citizens.

Further, the faulty assumption of Section 411 is that every terrorist organization uses every penny and every material good to further the ends of terrorism. David Cole gives the example of the Palestinian militant organization, Hamas. Israel says it only uses about 5% of its money on suicide bombings and violence. For that reason, the U.S. State Dept. in 1994 fought against membership in Hamas as a reason to deny visas.[26]

This Section also provides no hearing for aliens, only "reasonable grounds" on the part of the Justice Department to believe a terrorist connection exists. The Fifth Amendment "due process of law" in trials fits precisely here (i.e. the legal requirement that one is presumed innocent until proven guilty).

Section 411 also allows the government to present evidence to courts ex parte and ex camera (i.e. one-sided and no review permitted by their court opponent). This gives only lip service to a court of law, while stacking the deck in their own favor. It clearly does not permit defendants to "have their day in court," in the traditional sense of Fourth Amendment rights.

B. Section 412--Inflates the Attorney General's power to detain non-citizens for up to seven days without charging him/her with criminal or immigration violation charges. Also, immigration violations result in mandatory detention without release until the Attorney General determines they are not terrorists.

Furthermore, neither the Justice Department nor the INS is required to present evidence on the alien.

There are, again, several significant changes this provision makes. First of all, immigration policy is changed, making it much more restrictive. While this might be a natural and expected reaction of a government whose people have just been attacked, it might be argued that these restrictions are overreactions, since they even test a person's political affiliations as a ground of entry.

According to the Center for Constitutional Rights, the Due Process clause has been ruled by the Supreme Court to apply "to all persons within the United States, including aliens, whether their presence is lawful, temporary, or permanent."[27]

Also, there is a due process concern that is denied to immigrants under this section of PATRIOT, since the Attorney General may now detain them solely on his word that he has "reasonable grounds to believe" that such a person is engaged in terrorist activities.[28]

How does "Patriot II" violate due process?

Section 106 gives the target of illegal electronic surveillance no legal recourse.

Section 109—According to the ACLU, allowing the FISA Court to have contempt of court powers without due process is a violation of the Fourth Amendment, since it does not allow "a party facing a possible contempt sanction to appear before the Foreign Intelligence Surveillance Court and be heard, prior to the imposition of any sanctions."[29]

Section 503 eliminates all due process for immigrants.[30] Furthermore, as the ACLU's Timothy Edgar puts it,

> [u]nder this proposal, a non-citizen, including a lawful permanent resident, accused of posing a risk to national security, could be detained and deported without having committed any violation of the law and without ever knowing the basis of the accusation against him or her.[31]

VI. Free Speech (the First Amendment)

Contained in the First Amendment to our Constitution, it is one of our most cherished rights, traditionally. PATRIOT encroaches on that right in the following ways.

A. Section 218—permits surveillance of any "U.S. person" for any criminal investigation, as long as information gathered is for "a significant purpose." However, the Supreme Court has ruled, in U.S. v. U.S. District Court for the Eastern District of Michigan, that

official surveillance, whether its purpose be criminal investigation or ongoing intelligence gathering, risks infringement of constitutionally protected privacy of speech . . .
[because of] the inherent vagueness of the domestic security concept . . . and the temptation to utilize such surveillances to oversee political dissent.[32]

B. Section 411—Guilt by association (i.e. "engage in terrorist
activity") has been expanded here to providing any support for any organization designated terrorist, even retrospectively, by the government. "Terrorist organization" is also now defined as "two or more individuals, whether organized or not."

The Supreme Court has often ruled that aliens outside our
border—in contrast to aliens that live among us—have no constitutional rights. However, ideological exclusions such as in PATRIOT
raise Constitutional concerns. "The First Amendment is designed to
protect a wide-open and robust public debate," and if our government
can keep persons out of the country who espouse ideas they oppose, our
ability as Americans to exercise our First Amendment rights becomes
curtailed.[33]

More broadly, excluding people for their ideas is contrary to
the spirit of Freedom for which the U.S. stands.[34] The First Amendment
to the Constitution allows for peaceable assembly. Furthermore, according to Cole, the Supreme Court has ruled that the First Amendment
precludes "guilt by association" "because it penalizes individuals who
support only a group's lawful ends."[35]

C. Sections 215 & 505—issues gag orders on those visited by
the FBI

D. Section 412—allows detention and deportation of any immigrant who even verbally supports a terrorist organization.

E. Section 802—"domestic terrorism" is defined here as "acts
dangerous to human life that are a violation of criminal laws...[that]
appear to be intended...to influence the policy of a government by intimidation or coercion." This could well be used against protest groups,
as Nancy Chang points out.[36]

How does "Patriot II" violate free speech?

Section 120 & 121—The definition of terrorism, like that of
PATRIOT, could be used against any political protestor, from anti-war
demonstrators to anti-abortion protestors.

Section 206—Prevents grand jury witnesses from discussing
their testimony with anyone but their lawyer, in contradiction to the

usual protection afforded a witness by their First Amendment right to free speech.

Section 402-- Expands who may be arrested for providing material support to terrorism, even if it is done without intent to do so, and even if the organization being supported is not officially listed as a terrorist organization by the Department of Justice.

Section 411—in particular, this provision creates 15 new death penalties.

Could these criteria be used against protest groups, whose activities got out of hand and resulted in a death? The ACLU seems to think so.[37]

VII. Other Rights Issues Raised by PATRIOT and "Patriot II"

Whether you support or reject the PATRIOT Act as enhancing or detracting from human rights in America, the one thing that is agreed upon by all parties is that PATRIOT "breaks down the walls" between investigative agencies of the federal government such as the FBI, CIA, ATF, Secret Service, Defense Intelligence Agency, National Security Agency, and the Customs Service, all of whom now work together, and often now work under the same roof, with the same computer database, to do their intelligence and investigation work, as well as their prosecution work.[38] These walls were originally erected due to illegal domestic spying in the 1970's. The walls were designed to limit federal power. The supporters of this wall breaking done by PATRIOT claim that this allows the government to find terrorists in the United States much more easily. The detractors maintain that the walls that are really broken down are the separation between terrorism and regular criminal investigations. Both are accurate statements; the question is, do we need such a "breakdown of walls" to occur, and does this wall breaking constitute a threat to civil liberties?

Before examining the pro and con arguments involved in this complex issue, it is important to note what, in fact, PATRIOT has allowed in this area. First (and another way of putting the issue) is that, prior to PATRIOT, there was a clear distinction in the law between criminal investigations and foreign intelligence investigations. Under PATRIOT, that distinction no longer matters, and all investigations from any investigatory branch of the federal government (named above) may use the same data and share it with one another. Second, it makes it legal for these various federal agencies to use the material generated by the federal grand jury process. This allows prosecutors to share their information with, for instance, the CIA. Third, grand juries operate with top secrecy in their evidence gathering. By allowing the

CIA, FBI, and other federal agencies to use the grand jury information-gathering content and process, it drops a cloak of secrecy over all federal government investigative functions, for any criminal act, not just terrorism. Fourth, and perhaps most importantly, the removal of the wall between federal grand juries and intelligence agencies also removes oversight of this process by a federal judge. Because the function of the grand jury is to investigate criminal wrongdoing and even to clear the innocent of charges, it was given the ability to force secret testimony and to jail uncooperative witnesses.[39] Now, however, the function of the grand jury could widen to include simple intelligence gathering on U.S. persons, unrelated to any charges that would be made against them.

According to Christopher Wray, Assistant Attorney General of the Criminal Division of the Justice Department, the breaking down of the walls allowing information sharing to take place between agencies has enabled the Justice Department to have great success at arresting terrorist suspects.[40] This same argument was made by Patrick Fitzgerald, U.S. Attorney for the Northern Illinois District, at the same Senate Judiciary Committee hearing. Unfortunately, we have only to go on their word, for they were short on examples of how this is the case. Mr. Wray also argued that no wall-breaking provision of PATRIOT has been yet ruled unconstitutional.

In opposition to that, it is important to repeat that PATRIOT opens the information sharing between federal agencies to any criminal investigation, not simply terrorist investigations. In doing so, it threatens the privacy of American citizens.

According to C. William Michaels, the PATRIOT Act, particularly Title II, eliminates all barriers between surveillance, investigation, and information-gathering roles of the FBI and CIA. In doing so, "it brings the entire federal law enforcement and investigative apparatus into a free-flowing information stream . . . without any control aside from internal guidelines."[41] Equally important is that this information encompasses the whole spectrum of electronic communication, no matter what the means of communication is. Worse yet, PATRIOT allows nationwide surveillance to be done by these federal agencies with a single surveillance order, which they can get anywhere. Formerly, there were state and regional offices that had to be involved in clearing the way for such surveillance. One way or another, this concentrates a tremendous amount of power into a few hands at the federal level, to say nothing of a tremendous amount of information that is now at their disposal.

Furthermore, information of any type may be investigated, collected, and shared inter-agency, as long as foreign intelligence is "a purpose," not "the purpose" of the investigation. These warrants do not have to be based on probable cause. In particular, Section 203 opens the door for extensive information sharing between agencies covering "*nearly any existing federal law enforcement or investigative agency.* There are no limits on the timing, extent, or frequency of this information sharing."[42] Furthermore, there is no requirement in PATRIOT that "any notice of this sharing has occurred be filed by any government attorney in any court, as with grand jury information."[43] Nor is there a court order needed for such information sharing. Nor are these provisions restricted to immigrants.

What seems to be at issue here is not that the federal agencies did not have enough information to prevent 9/11 from happening. Rather, it seems to be the case that they did not get the information up the chain of command in timely and efficient manner. This problem would not necessitate the far-reaching expansions of power that PATRIOT provides the feds here.

The concerns mentioned in this discussion, and the ensuing debate, concern not just the sections of PATRIOT mentioned here; they also apply to Section 358 (allowing credit and consumer reports to be collected and shared inter-agency, without warrant and without probable cause); Section 403 (identification of immigrants by biometric [fingerprint, retina, etc.] and other background checks, to be shared inter-agency); Section 413 (allowing government information sharing with foreign governments); Section 504 (allowing information extracted from searches and seizures to be shared inter-agency); and Section 901 (allowing further Justice Department-CIA information sharing).

The legal matter involved also concerns the CIA charter, which bars if from domestic information gathering.

Another issue that is raising eyebrows is the very vague and general definition of "domestic terrorism" in PATRIOT, Section 802:

> Acts dangerous to human life that are a violation of the criminal laws . . . [and] appear to be intended . . . to influence the policy of a government by intimidation or coercion . . . [and] occur primarily within the territorial jurisdiction of the United States.

Also at issue in definitions are the definitions of "terrorist activity" as basically any use of violence by an immigrant; "terrorist activity" as doing anything that can be taken as support of "terrorism;" and "terrorist organization," as "two or more individuals, whether organized or not," which support "terrorism." These definitions are given in PATRIOT, Section 411, and are all extremely wide. There are many normal activities that can be taken as supporting terrorism in these definitions, including giving money to charity. If such an organization turns out to have been a terrorist one, designated by the Attorney General subsequent to ones providing "material support" for them, that person is presumed guilty of supporting terrorism unless they could prove that they were innocent; that is, "that he did not know, and should not reasonably have known, that the solicitation would further the organization's terrorist activity." These definitions cover nearly every political group in existence. As such, they constitute a potential threat to civil liberties, as the potential for abusing the definitions is virtually limitless.

Another issue that needs to be examined in the national debate on these pieces of legislation concerns the extreme curtailment of the Freedom of Information Act (FOIA), while at the same time dramatically increasing the ability of the government to collect massive amounts of information on U.S. persons. Both PATRIOT and II can be cited virtually ad infinitum concerning this issue (e.g. PATRIOT: Sections 213; 215; 216; 218; 505; 506; 508; DSEA: Sections 107; 109; 122; 124; 125; 201; 202; 311; 312).

Again, a critical issue is the lack of judicial overview or checks and balances concerning Justice Department activities. See, for example, what power the Attorney General creates for himself, without having to report to any overseeing judge or court, in PATRIOT, Sections 215; 216; 412; 505; DSEA, Sections 103; 123; 128; 204; 322.

Finally, there should be substantive discussion concerning the use of terrorism statutes and procedures, now applied to domestic criminal acts in PATRIOT, Sections 213; 411; DSEA, Sections 120; 121; 124; 129; 322; 411; 504.

In terms of actual rights violations which we have not covered in the sections above, these mainly apply to DSEA, as follows.

Section 405--The Eighth Amendment guarantees that excessive bail will not be required of a detained person. Yet this is precisely what is denied under this Section by engaging in preventive detention, and requiring the defendant to prove that s/he is not a threat to commit the Attorney General's laundry list of possible terrorist crimes.

Section 501—The Fourteenth Amendment states, in part, that "All persons born or naturalized in the United States and subject to the jurisdiction thereof, are citizens of the United States and of the State wherein they reside." The Supreme Court has repeatedly ruled that crimes do not entail loss of citizenship as part of punishment, even in times of war.[44] Rather, as Timothy Edgar puts it,

> expatriating acts must indicate some desire to show an affinity with a foreign government . . . [Thus] [p]roviding support to a terrorist organization, which possesses no sovereignty under international law, is a crime...but plainly does not indicate that the individual desires to attach himself or herself to the allegiance of a foreign nation or to abandon U.S. citizenship.[45]

Section 503—The Supreme Court has repeatedly ruled that

> the Due Process clause [of the Fourth Amendment] applies to all persons within the United States, including aliens, whether their presence here is lawful, unlawful, temporary, or permanent.[46]

Section 504—This section again denies due process, as well as habeas corpus rights, to noncitizens.

VIII. The Justice Department Replies to Critics

In 2003, the Justice Department set up a web site to respond to critics of the PATRIOT Act.[47] In what follows, we will examine each statement Mr. Ashcroft and his agents make on it, followed by a rebuttal.[48]

1. *"The PATRIOT Act limits domestic terrorism to conduct that breaks criminal laws, endangering human life. 'Peaceful groups that dissent from government policy' without breaking laws cannot be targeted."*

Under Section 215 of PATRIOT, the reference explicitly states that any "United States person" may be investigated so long as the investigation is not based on activities protected by the First Amendment. Furthermore, this statement of the Justice Department is misleading. Under PATRIOT, any group designated as a "terrorist supporter" by the Attorney General can be targeted for surveillance.

2. *"The PATRIOT Act specifically protects Americans' First Amendment rights, and terrorism investigators have no interest in the library habits of ordinary Americans."*

Section 215 of Patriot allows materials to be gathered without probable cause. All they have to do is state that the records are being "sought for" an ongoing investigation (ACLU). Furthermore, this is again misleading. This applies only to the target of the investigation and not to those whose records are being sought. Once an investigation is under way, any records on any citizen may be requested under PATRIOT, without showing any connection to criminal activity.[49]

3. *"The PATRIOT Act allows investigators to use the tools that were already available to [them] to investigate organized crime and drug trafficking."*

Once again, this is misleading. Intelligence gathering is not distinguished from criminal investigation in PATRIOT. While the latter activity certainly had tools available for use, the former activity on the part of the Justice Department did not. In other words, the subpoenas available for drug arrests are limited to criminal investigations and are public, whereas in Section 215 of PATRIOT, the requests have no connection to crime and are secret.[50]

Second, there were sweeping changes made to the law in PATRIOT (the following is all from the ACLU web site), including the following. PATRIOT empowers the FBI to obtain records of anyone at all, including people who are not suspected of involvement in criminal activity, and prohibits organizations that are forced to disclose their records from telling anyone about it (Section 215). It also empowers the FBI to ignore the probable cause requirement of the Fourth Amendment (Section 218). No law in history has ever done this. Third, it empowers the FBI to conduct searches in homes and offices without notifying the targets of searches until much later (Section 213). Finally, it expands the Attorney General's power unilaterally to demand the credit and banking records of anyone at all, including people not suspected of criminal activity (Section 505).

Third, the FISA court itself ruled 16 months ago that it is improper for federal authorities to mix intelligence information with criminal cases, as Patriot allows. But the Justice Department appealed that decision, and it was overturned by a secret appeals court. There was no opposing party in that court case, so no one was present to argue against the Justice Department's appeal.[51]

4. *"[Searching without warrant] allows law enforcement to conduct investigations without tipping off terrorists."*

FISA allowed such searches of "foreign powers and their agents." Second, Section 213 allows such warrantless searches for *any* criminal investigation (ACLU).

5. *"Section 215 allows government only to search business records."*

Section 215 authorizes the FBI to order any organization to turn "any tangible thing" over to the government. In a June, 2003, hearing before the House Judiciary Committee, the Attorney General himself admitted that under this provision, the FBI could seize personal belongings, educational and medical records, library records, and genetic information (ACLU).

6. *"The PATRIOT Act specifically protects Americans' First Amendment rights."*

This is misleading. First of all, Section 215 states that citizens and permanent residents can't be investigated based "solely" on the exercise of their First Amendment rights. Secondly, this applies only to the target of an investigation and not to those whose records are being sought in the investigation. Once an investigation is under way, any records on any citizen may be requested under PATRIOT, without showing any connection to criminal activity.[52]

7. *"The PATRIOT Act has led to crucial successes in the war on terrorism."*

First of all, Mr. Ashcroft's linkage of the Act to the indictments he has handed down is misleading. He claims to have brought 255 charges in terror investigations. However, a close look at those 255 shows that many were immigration violations, lying to an FBI agent, or credit card fraud.[53] Also, he claims to have deported 515 under PATRIOT, but he fails to mention that the Justice Department only allows deportation after the FBI has cleared the immigrants of involvement with terrorism (ACLU).

Second, Mr. Ashcroft is long on claims, but short on figures. When asked by Congress to substantiate such claims specifically, Ashcroft and his aides repeatedly claimed that such information was "classified." However, he did state that he had signed 170 emergency orders in a year and a half to allow electronic surveillance, allowed 47 searches in that same time without warrant, and contacted 50 libraries to ascertain information on patrons. When asked how many times federal agents had actually visited a library, one of Ashcroft's aides said: "Whether it is one or 100 or zero, the number is classified."[54]

8. *"The PATRIOT Act prohibits people leaking to the public the contents of private communications, and limits the use of Carnivore."*[55]

First of all, while "leaking" is prohibited, "information sharing" between government officials is expressly allowed in PATRIOT. Second, Carnivore technology can be easily abused as to security and safety of the people whose information it collects. Third, President Bush signed an executive order shifting the approval needed for use of Carnivore from the Assistant Attorney General's office to the field offices, which means easier use and less oversight.[56] Finally, there has been no attempt by the administration or the Justice Department to create an auditing trail that could be checked to see who is using Carnivore and for what purposes.[57]

IX. Other Objections and Replies

The following objections are statements either in print or in verbal form that call for a response.

1) *"We have to trust our government to protect us and not abuse their powers."*[58]

First of all, democracy is based on a "checks and balances" system, not on blind faith in pubic officials. Second, the founders of the country believed in the necessity of an informed and critical citizenship in order for democracy to work. Third, in June and again in July, 2003, the Justice Department's own Inspector General, Glenn A. Fine, released two different reports that were intensely critical of Justice Department's use of the law and of PATRIOT, especially regarding the detention of those arrested under PATRIOT.

2) *"If you do nothing wrong, you have nothing to fear."*

First of all, the Bill of Rights was enacted to prevent precisely this idea! It was created to prevent the fear of government intrusion when the citizen has done nothing wrong. If power can be abused, there is a good chance it will be.

Second, the presumption of American jurisprudence is that you are innocent until proven guilty, *not* suspected of being guilty and watched by your government until you prove yourself innocent.

Third, "wrong," in this context, is usually defined as synonymous with "illegal." However, PATRIOT allows "information gathering" instead of "investigating what is wrong" in someone's actions or words.

Fourth, "wrong" can be defined in very broad and most importantly, very *discretionary* ways by government officials. For example, "protest" can be considered "wrong" under USA PATRIOT.

3) *"We need to surrender or curtail some of our liberties for the goal of winning the war on terrorism."*

First of all, human rights are *inalienable* in *all* documents we have seen on them. Second, if rights are in fact dissolved or detracted from, the road back to them may be non-existent. Third, this is an ongoing war because there is no know enemy. Thus, to surrender rights, one would be more or less doing so on a permanent basis because the war will be perpetual.

4) *"There is a historical precedent to the surrendering of rights when we are attacked (e.g. World War II)."*

First, to assert a precedent does not legitimate a practice, ethically or legally. Second, there has been no historical precedent for this type of war, in which the enemy is largely unknown and not a nation-state, and which has already been characterized by the Bush administration as a war "with no end in sight." We began operations in Afghanistan and Iraq, with more said to be on the way in Syria, Iran, and/or North Korea. However, we have not yet stabilized the first two countries we have invaded. This "war," undeclared as a "war" by Congress, will be an extremely long one; one that we have not ever experienced before. Do we want to surrender our rights indefinitely and perhaps in perpetuity?

5) *"The PATRIOT Act will mean less spying, since it codified what was only common practice, and thus puts limits on the government surveillance, such as limiting email eavesdropping to subject lines only."*[59]

We have already seen the extensive information sharing issues caused by PATRIOT. More importantly, we have seen the very wide net PATRIOT casts over what may be taken as part of standard surveillance, and where it may be obtained (e.g. grand jury investigation processes). Furthermore, while it is true that there is now an updated law to reflect advances in technology, this still gives the government incredible leeway in what it is permitted to eavesdrop on, as we have also seen. Again, history shows that where the government has the opportunity to abuse its power, it will. This is exemplified in the illegal domestic spying of the 1960's and 1970's, which created the laws separating domestic from foreign spying to begin with. Moreover, even with some of the provisions of PATRIOT requiring approval for surveillance, we have seen that such approval is now available at local field offices, not from the "higher ups" of the Justice Department, thanks also to PATRIOT. This invites abuse at even the lowest levels of government surveillance. This would especially apply in cases where the "Carnivore" system is permitted use, since the content of emails is swallowed up by Carnivore, and the eavesdropping involves every ISP in the process of email communication. How well Carnivore can or will be used to separate out certain email content and persons from others on the same or even different ISP's is unclear at this point.[60]

6) *"PATRIOT doesn't stop people from protesting or criticizing Bush administration policies. One can see it happening regularly."*[61]

No one ever made this claim, so this is a straw man argument. Rather, the claim was that the First Amendment is being threatened by PATRIOT. We have seen this substantiated above.

7) *"Without civil libertarians to tell us of the alleged erosion of our civil liberties, most Americans would have never noticed a difference."*[62]

This is a red herring. The issue of the threat to civil rights has nothing to do with whether or not people notice that they are being threatened. This presumes, or at least implies, that rights come about, or only remain in force for so long as, the people are aware of them.

8) *"There is no threat to privacy in PATRIOT. The courts have long allowed police to postpone notification of searches when it might cause serious harm [e.g. terrorist plans]."*[63]

There are numerous threats to privacy, only some of which have been enumerated above.

9) *"Section 215 (on library spying) made only a modest change. Long before PATRIOT, a prosecutor during a grand jury session could inspect bank and library records without a court order."*[64]

While it is true that Section 215 requires a court order, what it does not require is probable cause for the warrant. Further, the judge hearing a government case under 215 is required to issue an order upon proper presentation of information by the government. Moreover, it imposes a gag order on persons who are contacted by the FBI. All of these are radical changes to current law, not "modest" ones.

10) *"PATRIOT requires a judge's approval for examination of library records in foreign intelligence cases."*[65]

This is true, but see above for the rest of what it requires.

11) *"In June of 2000, the National Commission on Terrorism reported that the FBI 'suffers from bureaucratic and cultural obstacles to obtaining terrorism information.' PATRIOT corrected that."*[66]

These are administrative, and as the report explicitly stated, bureaucratic problems. They did not require an Act of Congress to resolve. Rather, restructuring and reorganizing some of the top-heavy and slow bureaucracy within the federal system could well have ironed out many of the problems named by this report.

12) *"This is a most unusual war, but it is indisputably a war. And measures that would be indefensible during peacetime are often necessary and even urgent when the nation is grappling with a mortal threat. If we were fighting a conventional adversary, most of what the administration has done wouldn't be controversial."*[67]

Aside from some of the hysterical language employed here (e.g. no "war" has been declared by Congress, and the threat is not necessarily "mortal"), the essence of the objection here is that "tough times call for tough measures." This may be true, but there is no need to throw the Constitution out while doing so. If the threat is in fact "mortal," it is a threat against the very fabric of democracy in the United States: our liberty. There is no need to truncate it as extensively as the PATRIOT Act does to further the ends of fighting against terrorism. There are many weapons at our disposal, including international cooperation and reexamining our foreign policy. There is ample reason to maintain that, when compared to the philosophy of John Locke or to the Bill of Rights, the PATRIOT Act threatens the fabric of our society more than Osama bin Laden does. This will be discussed further in Chapter Five.

13) *"PATRIOT gives the U.S. government stronger tools with which to deter and disrupt terrorism."*[68]

It also gives the government the same tools for use on both any criminal action and on ordinary citizens, as we have seen. For this reason, it can be said that PATRIOT goes too far in what it allows. While the balance between the government pursuit of terrorists and maintenance of civil rights is a tricky one, we can see that PATRIOT goes too far in the direction of permitting government wide-ranging and secretive powers beyond what is necessary to fight terrorism. That is why the alarm is being raised by civil rights advocates. When joined with other Bush administration actions (which we will outline in Chapter Five), there is a serious threat to civil rights involved in PATRIOT. This, of course, is not meant to condemn all of PATRIOT. The statement by Russ Feingold, Democratic Senator from Wisconsin, is appropriate in this regard: "Not all of PATRIOT is bad, but the bad parts are fixable. So let's fix them." This is the proper course to take; not defend it carte blanche.

14) *"PATRIOT has allowed U.S. surveillance laws to update to the levels of current technologies."*[69]

This is true, but we have seen how far it goes in the direction of allowing eavesdropping on every facet of communication between U.S. persons. See Section VII above.

15) *"Terrorists now operate within the U.S., and in order to ferret them out, we need PATRIOT laws."*[70]

This is just another way of stating that the walls separating information sharing and allowing tapping into grand jury information and secrecy are necessary. We have dealt with this objection above.

16) *"There have been key successes in terrorist arrests as a result of PATRIOT."*[71]

This is true, but again, at what cost? If the cost is that we have surrendered part or much of our cherished democratic tradition of liberty and rights, then we have paid too much for the key successes involved. In a Utilitarian calculation of this sort, a prior good of democracy must be recognized as weighing more than simple pursuit and arrests of potential terrorists.

17) *"There are procedural safeguards being followed, as all actions taken under PATRIOT are reviewed by an independent federal judge."*[72]

As we have seen above, even if this has happened in the past, it need not happen as a result of PATRIOT, which allows extensive privilege and secrecy to Justice Department investigations. These characteristics include exclusion of the judiciary in many cases, and in others require the signature of the judge, who has no discretion in the matter at hand (which is the same thing as excluding the judiciary).

18) *"Issues like delayed warrant notification have been used, especially for drug-related arrests, for years."*[73]

The problem here is that the delayed notification allowed in PATRIOT has vastly expanded beyond the one case of drug arrests in three ways. First, such delayed warrant notification has been expanded to all criminal investigations, thus applying to cases in which it is surely not needed. Second, it expands the time frame for notification from the usual seven days to whatever "reasonable period" the Attorney General dictates. Mr. Ashcroft has already said that such notification can be considerably longer than the seven-day period.[74] Third, there is no sunset provision on this section of PATRIOT. Hence, the power of surveillance and arrest have been expanded exponentially, and one might argue, well beyond the reasonable range to fight terrorism

19) *"Single (nationwide) warrants allow bureaucratic delays to be avoided, thus allowing faster action with surveillance and arrests."*[75]

Such warrants also exclude judiciary processes, as we have seen above. In this respect, they should be treated as suspect when compared with the Fourth and Fifth Amendments.

As a final reflection for this chapter, perhaps it would do well to focus on the government definition of "terrorism" as contained in PATRIOT: any activities that "involve acts dangerous to human life that are a violation of the criminal laws" and which "appear to be intended" to "intimidate or coerce a civilian population" or "to influence the policy of a government by intimidation or coercion." What are the consequences that follow from this broad definition? First of all, the U.S. would have to condemn as "terrorist" the bombings of Hiroshima and Nagasaki, as well as U.S. support for governments in central America that killed thousands of civilians, as well as the direct attack on the Iraqi infrastructure in 1991 (e.g. water treatment facilities); U.S. support of Turkey, which has killed over 30,000 Kurds in a 15-year war, and created 2 million Kurdish refugees, and 10,000 political prisoners.[76]

Second, as we have seen, it is possible that this new definition of terrorism will adversely affect people who engage in acts of political protest. Also at risk is anyone who provides lodging to someone designated later a "terrorist." (e.g. a political protestor).

In conclusion, this text has been written in order to make a prima facie case that the USA PATRIOT Act, as well as the proposed "Domestic Security Enhancement Act of 2003," directly circumvent both the spirit as well as the letter of the United States Constitution. It is the hope of this author that this book can assist to wake the American people up from their slumber, before it is too late, and we find, upon waking, that our rights have disappeared, and we have become a totalitarian state. This consequence is not out the realm of possibility, and there are positive signs from our cities as well as our Congress, that people are indeed awakening to the dangers of these pieces of legislation. What makes America the great country it is, is not our military or our wealth, but our Constitution and our rights that are guaranteed by it. We continue to be a great country to the degree that we are committed to maintaining those rights for all.

Notes

1 Locke, *Two Treatises of Government*, op. cit., II, paragraph 57.
2 Ibid., paragraph 172.
3 Quoted in Chang, "The USA PATRIOT Act," op. cit.
4 Locke, op. cit., II, paragraph 135, and passim.
5 Ibid. paragraph 138.
6 Locke, op. cit., II, 17 and 23.
7 Ibid. II, VIII, esp. paragraph 97.
8 While it is true that Locke did not recognize the three part checks and balances system of contemporary American democracy (Legislative, Executive, and Judicial—Locke did not advocate the Judicial), nonetheless he is quite clear about the need for a limit on the Legislative powers, in Book II, chapters XI-XIII.
9 Ibid., paragraphs 135-139.
10 Ibid. paragraph 135.
11 Ibid. paragraph 138.
12 Ibid. paragraph 190.
13 For just a few of the specific legal cases one can cite in support of this contention, see Cole, ibid., pages 285-286.
14 See Chang, Lost Liberties, pp. 44-45.
15 Michaels, C. William. *No Greater Threat: America After September 11 and the Rise of a National Security State* (New York: Algora Publishing, 2002), page 61.
16 *Zadvydas v. Davis*, 533 U.S. 678, 690 (2001).
17 See Chang or Edgar, www.aclu.org, op. cit.
18 Edgar, Timothy H. "Section-by-Section Analysis of Justice Department Draft 'Domestic Security Enhancement Act of 2003,' also known as "'PATRIOT I'," www.aclu.org, February 14, 2003.
19 Actual quotation taken from http://www.righttoprivacy.com.
20 Chang, *Silencing Political Dissent*, p. 51
21 Ibid. p. 53.
22 Linda Monk, *The Bill of Rights: A User's Guide*, op. cit. p 130.
23 NAACP v. Claiborne Hardware Company (1982). Quoted in Chang, *Silencing Political Dissent*, p. 148.
24 David Cole, *Terrorism and the Constitution*, p. 155.
25 Ibid., p. 65. Cole cites the case of Brandenburg v. Ohio (1969).
26 Ibid., p. 155.
27 See Nancy Chang, "The USA Patriot Act: What's So Patriotic About Trampling on the Bill of Rights?," http://sss.ccr-ny.org/whatsnew/usa_patriot_act.asp.
28 See Nancy Chang, www.ccr-ny.org. "The USA PATRIOT Act: What's So Patriotic About Trampling on the Bill of Rights?"

29. Edgar, op. cit.

30 Edgar, op. cit.

31 ibid.

32 Chang, *Silencing Political Dissent*, p. 57.

33 Cole, *Terrorism and the Constitution*, p. 158.

34 Ibid.

35 Cole, David. Enemy Aliens (New York: The New Press, 2003), p. 60.

36 *Silencing Political Dissent*, p. 45.

37 ibid.

38 McGee, Jim. "In Federal Law Enforcement, 'All the Walls Are Down'," *Washington Post*, October 14, 2001.

39 Ibid.

40 C-SPAN, PATRIOT Act hearing before the Senate Judiciary Committee, 10/21/03.

41 Michaels, C. William, op. cit., page 67.

42 Ibid., page 51, emphasis his.

43 Ibid., page 52.

44 See ACLU, op. cit. Edgar uses the cases of Trop v. Dulles (1958) and Afroyim v. Rusk (1967). The former case concerns a court martial and the crime of desertion during WW II; that latter case concerns a citizen voting in a foreign election. In both cases, the Supreme Court ruled that such actions were not indicative of the intent of a citizen to surrender his citizenship; that it took more than those particular acts to voluntarily surrender one's citizenship.

45 Edgar, op. cit.

46 Zadvydas v. Davis (2001), quoted in Edgar, op. cit.

47 www.lifeandliberty.com.

48 The rebuttals contained herein are a combination of my own thoughts, in conjunction with the rebuttals made by the ACLU on their web site in July of 2003. Direct quotations from the ACLU web site will be followed by their acronym in parentheses in the text itself, rather than by endnote.

49 David Cole, "On the Road With Ashcroft," *The Nation*, September 22, 2003.

50 Ibid.

51 *Washington Post*, Sept. 8, 2003.

52 Cole, "On the Road With Ashcroft," op. cit..

53 Ibid.

54 Washington Post, op. cit.

55 Orin S. Kerr, law professor at the George Washington University Law School, quoted in Patricia Cohen, "9/11 Law Means More Snooping? Or Maybe Less?," *The New York Times*, September 7, 2002.

56 *New York Times*, Sept. 7, 2002.

57 Ibid.

58 This objection and the response to it are based on the ACLU web site, which posted both.

59 See Patricia Cohen, op. cit.

60 Ibid.
61 *The Chicago Tribune* printed a series of editorial supporting arguments for the PATRIOT Act, from November 2-23, 2003. This argument was taken from the November 2 editorial.
62 Ibid.
63 Ibid. November 5, 2003.
64 Ibid.
65 Ibid.
66 Ibid., November 9, 2003.
67 Ibid., November 16, 2003.
68 Wray, Christopher, Assistant Attorney General, Criminal Division of the Justice Department, on C-SPAN, PATRIOT Act hearing before the Senate Judiciary Committee, 10/21/03.
69 Ibid.
70 Ibid.
71 Ibid.
72 Ibid.
73 Paul McNulty, U.S. Attorney for the Eastern District of Virginia, on ibid.
74 See Chang, "The USA PATRIOT Act: What's So Patriotic About Trampling on the Bill of Rights?," op. cit.
75 Ibid.
76 For more on this, see FAIR newsletter

Chapter Four: Pending Legislation Involving Civil Rights

Flushed with power and discontented with the first congressional PATRIOT victory, the Attorney General has proposed a follow-up piece of legislation to the PATRIOT Act, entitled the "Domestic Security Enhancement Act of 2003," nicknamed "Patriot II." If that was not enough, congressional leaders from both sides of the aisle have also proposed additional legislation to give the government even more power to enter into the lives of U.S. persons. In this chapter we will examine the main legislative proposals forthcoming, beginning with the so-called "Patriot II" Act.

I. The Domestic Security Enhancement Act of 2003 (DSEA; a.k.a. "Patriot II")

In February, 2003, the Attorney General publicly released a new proposal that he would like to see made into law. Then on September 13, 2003, President Bush weighed in by publicly proposing and endorsing the "Domestic Security Enhancement Act of 2003."[1] What follows is not an actual bill, then, but a proposal that is now in the public forum. As of December, 2003, it has not been presented to Congress. It is important, however, to bring this proposal to public attention due to some of the stark measures it takes concerning the open exercise of civil rights in the United States.

Patriot II is divided into five "Titles," each of which is intended to expand federal governmental power, specifically the power of the Attorney General, in his attempts to gather information on U.S. citizens and aliens, as well as the ability of his Justice Department to punish any perpetrators found by such spying.

Title I, called "Enhancing National Security Authorities," is arguably the most power-expanding section of the proposed Act. In this Title, there are many noteworthy proposals concerning wide-ranging new governmental powers in comparison with the rights of citizens protected by the Constitution.

Section 101 of this Title includes an overturning of the FISA provision for probable cause. FISA does not require probable cause that the target of surveillance be engaged in criminal activity; all that is required is probable cause that the target be an agent of the foreign government. With that requirement lifted in Patriot II, there is a carte blanche the Justice Department seeks for wiretapping U.S. citizens and permanent residents.[2]

Section 102 expands who may be prosecuted as an "agent of a foreign power." Current law requires that anyone who engages in "intelligence gathering" that "involve[s] or may involve a violation" of federal criminal law, be classified as an "agent of a foreign power." This section expands that to classify as "an agent of a foreign power," any person who gathers intelligence, "regardless of whether those activities are federal crimes." Thus, anyone who the Attorney General determines is gathering information on the federal government may be labeled as an "agent of a foreign power" and be electronically monitored. Accordingly, this applies to any U.S. person, since the requirements of FISA that the person to be wiretapped be an agent of a foreign power is lifted in this section of the Act. Finally, Section 102 takes the standards of information gathering directed at agents of foreign governments and turns them on U.S. citizens, by allowing the government simply to "gather information" on a citizen without some evidence that their activities violate the law.

Section 103 of this Title is the first one of DSEA to eliminate the use of the U.S. court system for the purposes of increased governmental spying. The court through which the government usually obtains warrants for the use of electronic surveillance is called the Federal Intelligence Surveillance Court (FISC), established in 1978 by the Federal Intelligence Surveillance Act (FISA) for the sole purpose of hearing government requests for warrants for the surveillance of citizens. This is a top-secret court, consisting of eleven judges (up from seven, by virtue of the USA PATRIOT Act), which operates on the top floor of the Justice Department, under heavy guard. The judges of this court make their decisions in secret, and they are not accountable to other courts for their decisions. In their history, they have never rejected a government request for a warrant for surveillance activities. However, now, under Section 103 in Patriot II, the Attorney General eliminates the use of even the FISC for warrants for electronic surveillance and even for physical searches, either when Congress authorizes military action short of war, against another country, or the U.S. is attacked in such a way as to create "a national emergency." This unlimited power is good for fifteen days after such events occur. This section, then, significantly expands when the Attorney General may bypass Congress and engage in unsupervised wiretapping of U.S. citizens, by circumventing the authority of Congress to declare when such national war emergencies exist. Under Section 103, this determination will be made by the Attorney General, once the President has declared that an attack on the U.S. has been made.

Section 105 vastly expands the type of information the Attorney General may obtain on persons. Current law prohibits use of gathered information "for law enforcement purposes" unless the disclosure includes a statement from the Attorney General that such information cannot be used in a criminal proceeding. This section eliminates the requirement that the Attorney General personally declare that the disclosure of information gathered on someone is not usable in a criminal context. In other words, this section allows the disclosure of gathered information to any other government agency, whether of a criminal nature or not, and excuses the Attorney General from having to make this distinction.

Section 106 shields wiretappers from prosecution for what they do, provided they had authorization from a senior official to engage in electronic surveillance. This has at least two consequences. First, even in the event that a wiretap is illegal, the agent performing it would not be held legally accountable for it. Second, the target of such surveillance is given no legal recourse if s/he believes s/he has been unjustifiably targeted for surveillance. FISA had in place criminal penalties on any government agent who engages in illegal or unapproved electronic surveillance by FISA.[3] These penalties would be removed under Patriot II.

Section 107 eliminates even more restrictions on government spying. Current U.S. law places strict standards on the use of pen registers to gather information on U.S. persons. For foreign nationals, the government is permitted to use pen registers simply "to obtain intelligence information." However, for U.S. citizens, the pen register must only be used "to protect against international terrorism or clandestine intelligence activities." This section would eliminate all restrictions on the use of pen registers against U.S. citizens, and allow the government to use such registers simply for gathering "intelligence information." Section 216 of PATRIOT had already lowered the FISA standard to simply require a government official to certify that the information it would reveal is "relevant" to an investigation. Under Patriot II, this standard is lowered even further.

Section 109 expands the secret FISA Court's powers to those equal to a U.S. district court, including granting this court the ability "to enforce its orders, including the authority to impose contempt sanctions in case of disobedience." Thus, with this secret court, not only will there be no public information available about government surveillance, but added powers will be granted as well to the secret court.

Sections 120 and 121 expand the definition of terrorism beyond FISA, to include "criminal investigations" under "terrorist activities." This sweeping provision allows the federal government to arrest and prosecute U.S. citizens under a wider net, such that if their actions violate federal or state law, are potentially dangerous, and are intended to affect a government policy (the definition of "terrorism" under both PATRIOT Acts), they can be prosecuted as "terrorist" instead of "criminal" simply by using the criminal codes already in place. This gives the Justice Department a great deal of power over the lives of citizens who violate normal criminal laws.

Section 122 highlights more expanded governmental powers, for purposes of spying on citizens. This section allows the government to authorize "electronic surveillance without a court order in emergency situations," *and* allows the use of "pen registers and trap and trace devices without a court order in emergency situations." How such an "emergency situation" is to be defined and determined is left unstated. Perhaps more importantly, this section expands who may be wiretapped. Under FISA, only "agents of a foreign power" could be targeted for surveillance. Under Patriot II, the federal government would be permitted electronic surveillance of any U.S. person simply for domestic intelligence purposes. Furthermore, the normal time limits for any domestic surveillance under FISA would all be doubled: pen and trap and trace devices could be used on U.S. persons for 120 days instead of 60 days. Finally, this section restricts judicial overview of governmental actions to no more than one report from the Justice Department every thirty days.

Section 123 expands governmental power in at least four ways. First, this section extends the number of statutory time limits relating to periods of electronic surveillance or monitoring and searches in investigations of terrorist activities "from 30 days to 90 days."

Second, current U.S. law allows discretion by judges who issue such surveillance orders as to when a report is due to the court from the government on such surveillance. This section amends that judicial leeway and "would not allow reports to be required at shorter intervals than 30 days in investigations of terrorist activities." Thus the judicial oversight of electronic surveillance currently imbedded in the law would become very limited under Patriot II.

Third, current U.S. law allows government to delay notification of the courts of the its "accessing a person's stored electronic communications where specified 'adverse results' would result from the notification." This section changes that to allow "endangerment of national security as a specified adverse result that permits delaying notification." Again, this Section intends to severely curtail, if not eliminate, judicial oversight of Justice Department activities regarding U.S. persons.

Fourth, this section "extends the normal authorization periods for pen registers and trap and trace devices in investigations of terrorist activities from 60 days to 120 days."

Section 124 refers to the use of "Multi-function Devices," and seeks to expand federal governmental power by allowing eavesdropping on *any* of the functions an electronic device produces. It also permits search warrants for all information retrievable from any electronic device. Thus, under DSEA, no matter what you do, if you are a target of government surveillance, and if what you do is done electronically, the government will be permitted to monitor *all* of its contents not by probable cause that you are using such technology for criminal purposes, but by suspicion that you are otherwise engaged in criminal activity. Thus, for example, if you advocate insurrection in an email, this section allows the government to monitor all other electronic devices you own that could be used to send email messages, such as your telephone line or cell phone. Such information has already been used by the Justice Department for purposes outside of terrorist investigations (e.g. drug violations, credit card fraud, etc.). The stated purpose of this section of the act is to allows multiple function devices to have each of their multiple functions tapped for surveillance. However, it amounts to a carte blanche for electronic surveillance by the Justice Department, by making automatic their ability to eavesdrop on any device: "communications transmitted or received through any function performed by the device may be intercepted and accessed unless the order specifies otherwise."

Second, this section permits the courts which authorize such eavesdropping to operate outside their geographical district for the purpose of government information gathering.

Section 126 would enable the government to obtain credit reports on individuals on virtually the same terms that private entities may obtain them. In addition, "this provision would prohibit disclosing to a consumer the fact that law enforcement has sought his credit report." It would allow the government to obtain credit reports of any American citizen without their knowledge or consent, and without any judicial oversight in so doing.

Section 128 allows the Justice Department to write its own subpoenas. Current law requires the Justice Department to obtain subpoenas of individuals from a grand jury. This section allows what are called "administrative subpoenas" to be issued outside of the grand jury for "investigations involving domestic or international terrorism...It also would prohibit a subpoena recipient from disclosing to any other person...the fact that he has received a subpoena." Thus complete secrecy of Justice Department activities is maintained and guaranteed. An "administrative subpoena," also called "a national security letter," is one which expands governmental power in at least two ways. First, it allows any local field office of the FBI to write its own subpoena, with no judge or court needed to do so. Second, the recipient of such a subpoena would be forced by law to cooperate with a federal investigator. Under the Fifth Amendment to the Constitution, one may refuse to provide an FBI agent with materials requested. Under this section of Patriot II, a person would no longer be permitted to appeal to the Fifth Amendment as a reason not to cooperate.

Equally chilling is what information Section 128 allows the Justice Department to collect:

> In any investigation . . . [of] an offense involved in or related to international or domestic terrorism . . . the Attorney General may subpoena witnesses, compel the attendance and testimony of witnesses, and require the production of any records (including books, papers, documents, electronic data, and other tangible things that constitute or contain evidence) that he finds relevant or material to the investigation . . . The attendance of witnesses and the production of records may be required from any place in any State or in any territory or other place subject to the jurisdiction of the United States at any designated place of hearing.

If this was not bad enough, Section 129 sets up stiff penalties for people who do not comply with the administrative subpoenas issued by FBI officials. Specifically, not complying with such letters would now be "a misdemeanor punishable by up to a year in prison, but would be punishable by up to five years of imprisonment if the unlawful disclosure was committed with the intent to obstruct the terrorism or espionage investigation."

This section also expands the purpose of information gathering on the part of the government. Whereas current law only allows such extensive information gathering for the purpose of "international terrorism" or "terrorist activities," this section makes the argument that this is insufficient for intelligence, because it may not be clear that what is being hatched is a terrorist plot. Thus, it allows the Attorney General to create his own guidelines for what information should be collected and disseminated.

In a related vein, Attorney General Ashcroft announced that the Justice Department would begin to gather information on judges who give lighter sentences than those called for by legislative guidelines.[4]

Title II is intended to "Protect National Security Information." Like Title I, the main intent is to increase governmental power to collect information *while at the same time* becoming more secretive about their information-gathering processes and contents. We will highlight three such instances.

Section 201 suspends much of the application of the Freedom of Information Act (FOIA), by the following claims: "the government need not disclose information about individuals detained in investigations of terrorism until disclosure occurs routinely upon the initiation of criminal charges." The intent of this section appears to be that of enhancing the ability of the government to withhold information on suspected terrorists, whom the government has in their custody, by rejecting all applicability of the Freedom of Information Act to their activities in this regard.

Section 202 will come as a shock to environmentalists. This section puts new restrictions on the FOIA with regard to disclosure of information related to pollution. Current law requires companies that use potentially dangerous chemicals to release a "worst case scenario" report that specifies the consequences of releasing such chemicals into the surrounding community. This section refers to such laws as "a roadmap for terrorists, who could use the information to plan attacks." Thus, this section restricts access to such information under FOIA. Specifically, any member of the public who reads any such information must maintain it in a "read only" method (i.e. not to be copied, noted, or repeated to anyone), and only those who live or work in a geographical area likely to be affected by a chemical release will be permitted to read the "worst case scenario" report. These reports are currently available to any member of the public under FOIA.

Section 202 is very specific regarding the intent of the government not to release pollution information to the public: "Information that is developed by the Attorney General, or requested by the Attorney General . . . for the purpose of preparing the report or conducting a review under this clause, shall not be disclosed or released under the Freedom of Information Act." Under this section, any government official who communicates such information will be charged with committing a criminal offense.

Section 204 is another section intended to take the courts out of Justice Department activities. Under current law, the Classified Information Procedures Act gives courts discretion about whether or not to approve a government request for authorization to submit sensitive evidence ex parte (i.e. from one point of view). This section strips the power of the courts to use discretion in granting the government such permission, and *requires* the court to grant the government such a request.

Section 206 "make[s] witnesses and persons to whom subpoenas are directed subject to grand jury secrecy rules." In other words, this provision would strip the right of grand jury witnesses to make any comment outside of the court regarding information they have been subpoenaed to present.

Title III, "Enhancing Investigation of Terrorist Plots," is perhaps the most draconian part of DSEA. In this title, the Justice Department will be permitted to collect DNA samples from suspected terrorists, and place them in a DNA database. It also places limits on court involvement in governmental spying on citizens, and also vastly expands who may be said to relinquish their U.S. citizenship and thus be subject to arrest and deportation by the Justice Department. We will examine each of these categories of proposed legislation.

Section 302 and 303 both deal with DNA collection. Current law permits the FBI to collect DNA samples of persons *convicted* of certain crimes. This section amends that law to allow the government to collect DNA of persons "*suspected* of terrorism." This includes those associated with suspected terrorist groups, and noncitizens who have supported, in any way, any group designated by the government as "terrorist." Furthermore, it allows "the use of such means as are reasonably necessary to collect a DNA sample."

Non-cooperation with such government attempts will now be classified as a class A misdemeanor.

Section 303 allows the Attorney General to establish a DNA database of suspected terrorists, and *requires* ALL federal agencies "to give the Attorney General, for inclusion in the databases, any DNA records, fingerprints, or other identification information that can be collected under this subtitle." Furthermore, this section "allows the Attorney General to use the information to detect, investigate, prosecute, prevent, or respond to terrorist activities, or any other unlawful activities by suspected terrorists." It also allows the Attorney General to disseminate such information to any other governmental agency, federal, state, or local. It also allows the Attorney General to search information in numerous other databases to collect information on suspects.

Section 311 provides "authority for sharing of consumer credit information, visa-related information, and educational records of information with state and local law enforcement" and places a gag order on anyone who is required by investigators to turn over information on a target of an investigation. It does not limit the information shared to terrorism investigations.

Section 312 does a minimum of three things with regard to governmental surveillance activity. First, this section invalidates all agreements that were made between states and the federal government (called "consent decrees") that were designed to limit the government's power to gather information about individuals and organizations. This section claims that such agreements impede the efforts of the federal government to combat terrorism, and thus proposes to "immediately eliminate" them, in favor of the blanket ability of the government to collect information on citizens in any state, at any time.

Second, this section places limits on what a court can reward a plaintiff in any lawsuit against the federal government over surveillance issues. It also orders all courts not to make any ruling that would contradict the new surveillance powers mandated by PATRIOT I or requested by DSEA. Patriot II maintains that such laws, which were passed because of past police abuses, hamper the federal government's efforts to stop terrorism.

> [Regarding] prospective relief in any civil action . . . The court shall not grant or approve any prospective unless the court finds that such relief is narrowly drawn, extends no further than necessary to correct the violation of the Federal right, and is the least intrusive means necessary to correct the violation of the Federal right. The court shall give substantial weight to any adverse impact on national security, public safety, or the operation of a criminal justice system caused by the relief...The court shall not order any prospective relief that requires a government official to refrain from exercising his authority under applicable law.

Third, this section allows any court reward to a citizen to be terminated immediately

> if the prospective relief was approved or granted in the absence of a finding by the court that the relief is narrowly drawn, extends no further than necessary to correct a current and ongoing violation of the Federal right, and is the

least intrusive means necessary to correct the violation of
the Federal right.

This means that, should the government determine that the court ruling
was not in line with the "narrowly drawn" provisions for "relief" to an
offended citizen, the court ruling could be invalidated.

Section 313 protects all businesses who report suspicious activities of their employees to the federal government, making them im-
mune from prosecution for engaging in such activities. This protects
businesses that voluntarily provide information to the federal government, even if that information is false, from being sued for defamation
by the target of the government surveillance.

Section 321 authorizes the Justice Department to wiretap U.S.
persons at the request of a foreign government, an activity not permitted by current law unless the U.S. Senate has approved a treaty with
such a country in advance of such requests. Even without such a treaty,
there is still ample provision for such requests from a foreign government.[5]

Section 322 is entitled "Extradition without Treaties and for
Offenses Not Covered by an Existing Treaty." There are four issues
pertinent to the new governmental power that would be given here.

First, this section expands the power of the federal government to extradite U.S. persons for various offenses, such as "distribu-
tion, manufacture, importation or exportation of a controlled substance,
computer crimes, money laundering, or crimes against children." Extradition under DSEA would be for "probable cause," not conviction of
a crime. Such offenses that permit extradition under Patriot II are to be
permitted whether or not the U.S. has a treaty with another country regarding such extradition practices.

Second, critical to this section is a subsection which allows extradition for "political offenses." This term remains undefined in Patriot
II.

Also critical to this section is a subsection which rules out
"humanitarian concerns" as reasons for not extraditing a person. It also
rules out court use of "the nature of the judicial system" or "whether
the foreign government is seeking extradition of a person for the purpose of prosecuting or punishing the person because of the race, religion, nationality or political opinions of that person" in reaching a decision regarding extradition from the U.S.

The fourth critical aspect of this section is the following critical clause: "The authorities and responsibilities set forth in this subsection are not subject to judicial review." Again, the court system is taken

out of the loop regarding Justice Department determinations of penalties. This denial of due process in court is also stated in Section 409, concerning the denial of certificates for civil aviation for national security reasons.

Title IV, "Enhancing Prosecution and Prevention of Terrorist Crimes," expands definitions of "terrorist activity" and the power of the Justice Department to pursue prosecution of people so designated under the proposed new rule. Section 402, for instance, under the title "Providing Material Support to Terrorism," explicitly criminalizes association with terrorist groups even if one had no intent to engage in specific terrorist criminal activities:

> this section amends the definition of 'international terrorism' to make it clear that it covers acts which by their nature *appear* to be intended for the stated purposes. Hence, there would be no requirement [on the part of the government] to show that the defendants actually had such an intent. (emphasis mine)

Thus, a person who gives money to an organization which is not officially labeled a "terrorist organization" by the federal government could still face prosecution by the Justice Department under this Section.

Section 404 mandates that any person who uses any electronic device with encryption technology to commit a crime is to "be imprisoned for an additional period of not fewer than 5 years." This type of technology is a standard part of many computer programs. This would apply to any federal crime, not just those of terrorism.

Section 405, "Presumption of Pretrial Detention in Cases Involving Terrorism" denies bail to persons charged with conduct which fits "a standard list of offenses that are likely to be committed by terrorists." There are none of the usual requirements that the government prove that the arrested person is a threat to public safety or that they might not show up at their trial. The "presumption," as stated in the title itself, is against the defendant.

Section 408, "Postrelease Supervision of Terrorists," changes two parts of the supervision law. Under the USA PATRIOT Act, there is the potential for lifelong supervision of persons released from prison after serving time for terrorist activities, with the limitation that the offense committed was one which caused "a foreseeable risk of death or serious injury." Under this section of DSEA, this is wiped away, and any person who is convicted of terrorist activities, even nonviolent ones, is subject to lifelong supervision. This includes those who are convicted of "support" of terrorism. This provision does this by mandating that any act which does *not* "create a foreseeable risk of death or serious injury," and is "in the standard list of crimes likely to be committed by terrorists" is liable for prosecution and mandatory lifetime supervision. Second, DSEA would change the law to allow a maximum reimprisonment sentence for violations of supervision. Third, the DSEA (specifically, in section 410) explicitly eliminates the statute of limitations for such offenses.

Section 411 widely expands the use of the death penalty to include any act that the government deems a "terrorist act" that results in death (intent is not mentioned in this section, so there are no judicial degrees for penalties where death results, such as in, for example, "second degree" murder), and any material support provided for such an act. As we saw in our examination of FISA and PATRIOT, these offenses include "acts dangerous to human life, that are in violation of state or federal law, and are committed in order to influence government by intimidation or coercion." This encompasses wide-ranging criteria and thus a wide-ranging application of the death penalty by explicitly referring to crimes "likely" to be committed by terrorists..

Subtitle B of Title IV is entitled "Incapacitating Terrorism Financing," and expands governmental authority over financial transactions that occur in business and/or those involving U.S. persons. Section 421 increases the current legal penalties for violating U.S. laws regarding economic exchanges with other countries to five times their current penalty (i.e. from $10,000 per offense to $50,000 per offense).

Section 422 focuses on "hawalas," an economic practice used in Arab cultures. The best way to define this practice, as well as the proposed law in response to it in Patriot II, we will quote the example presented in the Act itself, along with the Attorney General's proposed solution:

> [Person] A sends drug proceeds to [person] B, who deposits the money in Bank Account 1. Simultaneously or subsequently, B takes an equal amount of money from Bank Account 2 and sends it to A, or to a person designated by A. The first transaction from A to B clearly satisfies the proceeds element of the money laundering statute, but there is some question as to whether the second transaction—the one that involves only funds withdrawn from Bank Account 2—does so . . . This proposal is intended to remove all uncertainty on this point by providing that *all constitute parts of a set of parallel or dependent transactions involve*

criminal proceeds if one such transaction does so. (emphasis mine)

Section 423 revokes the tax-exempt status of any organization that the government deems to be associated with terrorism, in addition to continuing the practice of freezing their assets and preventing the member of the organization from entry into the United States.

Section 427 allows the federal government to seize the property of "any person planning or perpetrating an act of terrorism against a foreign state or international organization while acting within the jurisdiction of the United States." The definition of "terrorism," as throughout Patriot II, is the one used in the USA PATRIOT Act.

Title V, "Enhancing Immigration and Border Security," Section 501, "Expatriation of Terrorists," is the section that has sent waves of shock and alarm across the spectrum of civil liberties advocates, because it deals with citizens allegedly surrendering their citizenship. This section expands the category of those who the federal government can take as having renounced their U.S. citizenship, and therefore are susceptible to deportation. Current U.S. law states that a U.S. citizen can renounce their citizenship voluntarily by: 1) obtaining nationality in a foreign state; 2) taking an oath of allegiance to a foreign state; 3) serving in the armed forces of a foreign state that are engaged in hostilities with the U.S.

Patriot II expands this category to allow the government to expatriate any U.S. citizen who, *by inference from their conduct*, the government believes has in fact renounced their citizenship. This includes such activities as "becoming a member of, or providing material support to any organization" that the government claims is a "terrorist organization," and has "engaged in hostilities against the United States." Again, the determination of what defines a "terrorist organization" and what makes for "hostilities" remains unclear and not defined here. The serious rights issue here is that traditionally, one is said to expatriate oneself only if one has shown by his/her actions that s/he has made "a decision to accept [foreign] nationality." The Attorney General quotes this very case from a 1972 Supreme Court ruling, yet turns right around and asserts that this section of Patriot II "would make service in a hostile army or terrorist group prima facie evidence of an intent to renounce citizenship."[6] This Supreme Court ruling makes no mention at all that someone who supports a terrorist organization demonstrates a renunciation of citizenship, as this section seeks to make into law. Even more, the renunciation clause contained in DSEA does not limit itself to support of foreign terrorist organizations; it allows for the Justice Department to designate support of a domestic organization, branded by them as "terrorist," to be a cause for citizenship renunciation from its domestic supporters.

Section 502 increases the penalties for crimes committed by illegal immigrants to the U.S. under the pretext of connecting them to terrorism. This part of the proposed legislation has nothing at all to do with terrorism; rather, it is a clandestine attempt by the Justice Department to change immigration laws.

Section 503, "Inadmissibility and Removability of National Security Aliens or Criminally Charged Aliens," continues what Section 502 started, by giving the Attorney General the authority to bar an immigrant from entering the U.S., *or* to remove said immigrant, if "the Attorney General has reason to believe would pose a danger to the national security of the United States." Also, "The Attorney General in his discretion may at any time execute any order" with respect to barring entry of a person into the U.S. Part of what this section allows is for the Attorney General to grab authority that is equal to that exercised by the Secretary of State. Mr. Ashcroft himself admits this in the proposal. All that is needed is a statement alone from the Attorney General that the immigrant he wishes to deport "poses a danger to national security."

Section 504, "Expedited Removal of Criminal Aliens," expands who may be deported from the U.S., "to include all aliens, not just nonpermanent residents." This means that permanent residents of the United States would be subject to deportation if they committed a crime. It also expands the categories under which someone may be deported by the Attorney General to include "possession of controlled substances, firearms offenses, espionage, sabotage, treason, threats against the President, violations of the Trading with the Enemy Act, draft evasion, and certain alien smuggling crimes."

Most importantly, this section *removes the possibility for an immigrant to appeal* an order to leave the U.S. by the Attorney General. Thus, all cases the Attorney General places under this section have the right of habeas corpus stripped from the immigrant.

Section 505: "Clarification of Continuing Nature of Failure-to-Depart Offense, and Deletion of Provisions on Suspension of Sentence," does two things: it expressly states that any person given the order of deportation by the Attorney General must depart the U.S. within 90 days. Second, it "eliminates the authority of courts . . . to suspend for good cause the sentence of an alien convicted of failure to depart."

Section 506: "Additional Removal Authorities," gives all power to the Attorney General for determination of the place of deportation, "whether the country or region has a government, recognized by the United States or otherwise."

Section 506 permits the Attorney General to deport an immigrant to any country in the world, whether there is a current operative government there or not, and whether or not the United States diplomatically recognizes a government in a given country.

There are clear civil rights issues that Patriot II raises. When combined with the other legislative proposals forthcoming from some of our representatives, the effect is not only positively chilling, but is enough to make one wonder what is happening to our democracy. It is in the interest of preserving our rights-based democracy that the following proposals are highlighted.

II. Other Forthcoming Legislation and Governmental Programs That Concern Civil Liberties in Post-9/11 America

On September 9, 2003, Senator Orin Hatch of Utah proposed two pieces of legislation regarding the PATRIOT Act. The first was an attempt to repeal all the sunset provisions in PATRIOT.[7] Failing that, he has proposed legislation that he is calling "The Victory Act." According to Dan Eggen of *The Washington Post*, this proposal would

> dramatically expand the government's power to seize records and conduct wiretaps in connection with 'narcoterrorism' investigations . . . [expand] prosecutorial power in traditional drug cases...give the government more latitude to freeze assets of alleged drug traffickers or terrorists; make it easier to charge drug defendants with aiding terrorists, and loosen the standards used to convict defendants of laundering money.[8]

If this wasn't bad enough, Senators Jon Kyl, Republican of Arizona, and Charles E. Schumer, Democrat of New York, have proposed legislation that would "eliminate the need for federal agents who seek secret surveillance warrants to show that a suspect is affiliated with a foreign power or agent, or a terrorist group."[9] Called the "Kyl-Schumer Bill," it was revealed on Sept. 9, 2003, and was passed unanimously by the Senate Judiciary Committee.

The third thing we must be aware of in our post-9/11 country are two particular programs instituted by the government to collect information on U.S. citizens. The first of these programs is called "Total Information Awareness," and is designed to pull together as much information as possible about as many people as possible into an "ultra-large-scale" database, making that information available to government officials, who may sort through it at anytime to try to identify terrorists. According to the ACLU, this program would gather information on every person, including "medical records, financial records, political beliefs, travel history, prescriptions, buying habits, communications (i.e. phone calls, emails, and web surfing), school records, personal and family associations, credit card bills, etc."[10] There is even an attempt being made to develop a computer program called "LifeLog," which will capture the name of every TV show you watch and every magazine you buy.[11] In addition, already in testing mode, is a program entitled CTS ("Combat Zones that See"), blimps used to record movement of people, including license plates, facial features, and gait, keeping them in a central data bank. The goal, as a Pentagon spokesman said in a presentation to defense contractors, is to "track everything that moves."[12]

Finally, it is important to be aware of the program called CAPPS II. Proposed by the Transportation Security Administration (TSA), its real name is "Computer Assisted Passenger Pre-Screening System," and its purpose is related to TIA. It is a program that would collect every bit of information available on those who purchase airline tickets, create profiles on those who fly, and keep them in a central government database. This database would be available to local, state, federal, and international law enforcement officials.[13]

There are some serious problems with both TIA and CAPPS II. Perhaps most importantly, it replaces the longstanding jurisprudential tradition in the United States of the presumption of innocence, with suspicion. Governmental data collecting is usually only justified, legally or ethically, where there is evidence of involvement in wrongdoing. Aside from that, such a program would effectively end privacy as we know it by allowing the government to maintain extensive information bases on its citizens. If the right to privacy is to remain a constitutionally protected right, such programs as TIA and CAPPS II cannot co-exist with such a right, as they are contradictory ideas.

Furthermore, possible abuses are legion. For example, the Detroit Free Press reported that police officers with access to a database for Michigan law enforcement used it "to help their friends or themselves stalk women, threaten motorists, track estranged spouses, and intimidate political enemies."[14]

Most puzzling to this writer, such a program assumes that there are telltale patterns of terrorist behavior. From these "patterns," a profile is created, and every person is then judged according to the pattern. But if such patterns turn out to be wrong or woefully incomplete or inadequate, then the program itself is not only a waste of time and resources, but a dangerous intrusion on citizen privacy. In conjunction with this, such programs as TIA and CAPPS II record only electronic transactions. We already have learned that al Qaeda has revamped its communication procedures to exclude such lines of communication, so how effective could such a violation of privacy be?[15]

We have not seen an end to such legislative proposals and governmental programs. It is important, now more than ever, to be aware of the activities of our government. They are certainly becoming aware of ours! The next chapter will summarize some of the latest news on governmental actions and citizen responses to them.

Notes

1 Lichtblau, Eric, "Bush Seeks to Expand Access to Private Data," *The New York Times*, September 14, 2003.

2 Edgar, Timothy H. "Interested Persons Memo: Section-by-Section Analysis of Justice Department Draft 'Domestic Security Enhancement Act of 2003, also know as 'Patriot Act II,'" February 14, 2003, www.aclu.org/news.

3 Ibid.

4 Cronkite, Walter, "The New Inquisition," *The Denver Post*, September 21, 2003.

5 Edgar, op. cit.

6 The Supreme Court case in question is King v. Rogers, in which the Court ruled that "[S]pecific subjective intent to renounce United States citizenship...may [be] proved...by evidence of an explicit renunciation, acts inconsistent with United States citizenship, or by affirmative voluntary act[s] clearly manifesting a decision to accept [foreign] nationality."

7 Lichtblau, Eric, "Republicans Want Terror Law Made Permanent," *The New York Times*, April 9, 2003.

8 Eggen, Dan, "GOP Bill Would Add Anti-Terror Powers," *The Washington Post*, August 21, 2003.

9 Lichtblau, ibid.

10 ACLU, "Total Information Compliance: The TIA's Burden Under the Wyden Amendment," May 19, 2003, page 1.

11 Schachtman, Noah, "The Pentagon's Plan for Tracking Everything That Moves," *The Village Voice*, July 9, 2003. See also *The Chicago Tribune* editorial, "Security and Liberty in the Balance," June 9, 2003.

12 Ibid.

13 ACLU, "Questions and Answers on the Pentagon's 'Total Information Awareness,'" at aclu.org

14 Detroit Free Press, December 2001, as reported in ibid.

15 For these and more criticisms on these programs, see ibid.

Chapter Five: From PATRIOT to Police State? The Bush-Ashcroft Power Grabs

If the pieces of legislation we have examined were not enough to raise questions concerning the state of civil rights in America, the actions of President Bush and Attorney General John Ashcroft in the three years since the passage of PATRIOT should alert even the remaining skeptics that something is beginning to go very wrong with our form of democracy in Washington. If John Locke is correct when he said that those who would take the freedom of the people put themselves in a state of war with those whose freedom they are attempting to take, and the Bill of Rights is the fundamental expression of freedom, and the essence of American democracy and culture is about freedom, then the war on terrorism is not the only war the Bush administration is fighting.[1] The largely successful attempts of the Bush-Ashcroft team to consolidate power by limiting liberties far beyond what is necessary to fight terrorism will be documented below. The chapter will close with a reflection concerning the hubris involved in such power grabs. The events recounted below are in categorical, not chronological order.

I. Watching Congress

Perhaps the most significant of all news in the latter part of 2003 was the passage of the "Otter Amendment" by the House, by a vote of 309-118, on July 22, 2003. Its purpose was to de-fund Section 215 of the PATRIOT Act, specifically the parts allowing for government entrance into homes and businesses when there is no basis for suspecting criminal activity, as well as the part allowing government surveillance into bookstores and public libraries.[2]

Other Amendments to watch for include the following:[3]

1. The "Freedom to Read Protection Act" from Rep. Bernard Sanders, this bill repeals provisions of PATRIOT that subvert library patrons' privacy.

2. "Protecting the Rights of Individuals Act" from Senators Lisa Murkowski and Ron Wyden, which requires FBI agents to convince a judge of the merits of their suspicions before obtaining an individual's medical or Internet records.

3. "Library, Bookseller and Personal Records Privacy Act." This allows FBI access to business records pertaining to suspected terrorists or spies only.

4. "Security and Freedom Enhanced (SAFE) Act of 2003." This legislative proposal, submitted by Senators Larry Craig (R-ID) and Richard Durbin (D-IL), would rein in the PATRIOT Act's more egregious trampling on civil liberties, by doing the following. First, it would protect the privacy of personal medical, financial, library, and employer records by holding the Justice Department to the requirement of "specificity" of the Fourth Amendment. This requirement means that the Attorney General would have to have "articulable suspicion" that the records he or his agents seek belong to a spy or a terrorist.[4] Second, it would require the government to provide three specific reasons for delaying notice of a search warrant. Those three reasons are preserving life and safety, preventing flight from prosecution, or preventing destruction of evidence.[5] Third, it would limit "roving wiretaps" to the conditions that the government must know who is being tapped and what telephone device that suspect is using. Finally, it would add sunset provisions to parts of the PATRIOT Act that are not currently set to expire. Those sections are 213, 216, 219, and 505.

5. The House of Representatives approved the 2004 Intelligence Authorization Bill by a margin of 263-163. This legislation permits the FBI to demand records from businesses without court order, if it states that they are "relevant to a counter-terrorism investigation."[6]

6. On December 12, 2003, ten House Democrats requested sweeping congressional hearings on how the Justice Department has made use of the USA PATRIOT Act.

7. A very chilling Act before Congress is the "Intelligence Authorization Act of 2003," which expands the ability of government to "force financial institutions to disclose sensitive information about their customers without any judicial review or oversight."[7] All that would be required is for an agent to use a secret National Security Letter, which, thanks to the USA PATRIOT Act (Section 505), no longer requires individual suspicion that someone is involved with any criminal activity. According to the ACLU,

> This bill would allow government agents, such as the FBI, to access your personal travel records, stock trades or personal purchases without any suspicion that you were involved in a crime.[8]

It would also allow the government to maintain this surveillance in total secret, and without court involvement or knowledge.

II. Watching the Executive

Attorney General John Ashcroft instructed federal government agency heads to withhold information requested under the Freedom of Information Act (FOIA), assuring them that the Justice Department would support them in their practice. This concern with secrecy has been the modus operandi of the entire Bush administration since it took office. Not only has the administration sought to avoid releasing information about its activities to the public, but they have also attempted to avoid judicial review of their actions. For example, the Bush administration has issued numerous executive orders to get the power it wants when Congress denies them their wants.[9] The administration also maintains that the courts lack jurisdiction to rule on their designating U.S. citizens as "enemy combatants." As we have also seen, both USA PATRIOT and Patriot II limit or even exclude the courts from overseeing the actions of the administration, particularly the Justice Department. There have been numerous court battles over the withholding of information on the part of the Department of Justice, with varying results.[10]

In addition to the obsession with secrecy on the part of the administration and the Justice Department, there are serious reasons to be concerned with the attempts on the part of the federal government to diminish or even demolish the privacy rights of U.S. persons.[11] Perhaps Reg Whitaker summarizes it best in his article "After 9/11: A Surveillance State?" when he submits evidence that

> The daily lives of people . . . are now tracked and recorded. Electronic eyes scan the glove, from closed-circuit cameras on the ground, to satellites gathering sophisticated imagery from space. Voice communication is scooped out of the sky by electronic listening posts. Sophisticated search engines troll through e-mail traffic and Internet use. The global positioning system based on satellites can yield the precise location of targeted individuals anywhere on earth. Unique biometric identifiers, such as palm- and fingerprints, iris patterns, facial and gait characteristics, and DNA sequencing, are increasingly being recorded and stored in data banks . . . Virtually every daily economic transaction adds to an electronic trail that can potentially reconstruct a unique social profile of an individual. Detailed medical records and significant genetic information can profile individuals in a remarkably intimate manner.[12]

The problem is how to control such technology so that information does not fall into the wrong or unwarranted hands. Prior to 9/11/01, there were legal restrictions on the government usage of such information. As Whitaker has shown, however, the USA PATRIOT Act breaks down a significant number of those legal restrictions on the privacy of U.S. persons.[13] In addition to this legislation, the FBI has instituted a program called "Carnivore" which may "absorb" all the data of any communications device of any person, for storage in a databank. This program records all numbers dialed, web sites visited, and content taken, from any Internet Service Provider (ISP) network. It takes information from all users of the ISP it is attached to, not just those who are being investigated. Furthermore, the Homeland Security Act, signed into law by the President in November of 2002, permits ISP persons "voluntarily to provide government agents with access to the contents of private communications without those persons' consent, based on a 'good faith' belief that an emergency justifies the use of that information."[14]

Finally, the principle author of the USA PATRIOT Act, Viet Dinh, has recently expressed his reservations regarding how the Act is being used. Specifically, he has taken the stand that the government's arrest and detention of Jose Padilla would not stand in a court of law. Other former Justice Department officials have expressed similar concerns.[15]

III. Watching Lawsuits Over PATRIOT
Some lawsuits to watch include:

1. An ACLU suit under FOIA (Freedom of Information Act) to get information on how Justice Department was using PATRIOT was denied by the courts on May 19, 2003.[16]

2. The ACLU suit filed on August 5, 2003, over the use of PATRIOT to secretly seize business records in terror investigations.[17]

3. The Center for Constitutional Rights has filed a suit in Los Angeles federal court, challenging the entire constitutionality of USA PATRIOT.[18]

4. The ACLU, Americans for Tax Reform, American Conservative Union, Free Congress Foundation; Eagle Forum, and six Muslim groups filed a joint lawsuit over constitutionality of PATRIOT, Section 215, on July 30, 2003.[19]

5. On Thursday, December 18, 2003, two separate federal appeals courts ruled against the contentions of the Bush administration that the U.S. military may hold prisoners in terrorist cases in-

definitely, incommunicado, without access to lawyers, and without their cases being heard by American courts. The cases at issue in these rulings concerned the 660 prisoners being held at Guantanamo Bay, Cuba, and the U.S. citizen Jose Padilla, discussed above.[20]

IV. Watching Our Communities React to PATRIOT

Here is the latest regarding what U.S. cities and states have said and done regarding the USA PATRIOT Act:

1. Over 300 cities nationwide have passed resolutions opposing the PATRIOT Act, in whole or in part.

2. Chicago passed a watered-down version on October 2, 2003. The resolution on the table demanded lawmakers repeal the entire PATRIOT Act; the resolution that passed instead asked Congress to repeal those portions of PATRIOT that "violate fundamental rights and liberties."[21]

3. Three states—Vermont, Hawaii, and California—have passed resolutions condemning PATRIOT.

V. Watching the Watchers

The pivotal figure in the writing and use of the PATRIOT Acts, I and II, is the Attorney General himself, John Ashcroft. Here is what he and his boss, President Bush, have been doing lately.

1. In 2003, Ashcroft embarked on a "PATRIOT Rocks" tour of U.S. This is a closed-door program given to select U.S. cities, conducted *only* in front of law enforcement personnel and politicians already in favor of it, *while being closed to the public.* For example, in Boston, Ashcroft addressed 150 law enforcement officers and specially invited guests, while 1200 citizens, who waited outside in protest, were not permitted entry.[22] He has engaged no one in debate, and has not addressed the concerns of civil libertarians about his actions, particularly the PATRIOT Act.

2. Far more important than Mr. Ashcroft's U.S. promotional tour are the uses of USA PATRIOT for non-terrorist investigations and arrests. Some of the information that has been reported so far includes:

a. In a report presented to Congress by the Justice Department, the Department admitted to using PATRIOT in hundreds of cases outside of terrorist investigations, including investigation of drug traffickers, white-collar criminals, credit card theft, embezzlement, blackmailers, child pornographers, money launderers, and corrupt foreign leaders.[23]

b. The Justice Department is now using PATRIOT to seize millions of dollars in foreign banks that do business in the U.S.[24]

c. The FISA Court publicly identified more than 75 cases under PATRIOT in which the FBI lied to or mislead them in its requests for electronic surveillance of Americans. These requests were "not reasonably designed" to safeguard the privacy of Americans, the court said.[25]

3. Prominently reported cases of abuse under PATRIOT so far include the following:

a. San Jose, California—May, 2003—French Clements graduated from college and tried to open an online brokerage account with Harrisdirect, where his stepfather has an account. The day after he completed his application, he received an email from them, stating: "We regret to inform you that we are unable to approve your application at this time; the customer's identity not properly authenticated per the USA PATRIOT Act."[26]

b. Andrew O'Connor of St. Johns college in Santa Fe, New Mexico, was removed from the library by police after he made negative comments about President Bush in an online chat room. He was released without being charged, but police are not answering reporters' questions about how they knew what he was saying.[27]

c. A New Jersey library patron called the police from his cell phone to report that there was another patron reading something in a foreign-language web page on a computer. The man was arrested, not permitted to call home or lawyer, and then released without being charged.[28]

d. On May 8, 2002, Jose Padilla, an American citizen, was arrested at Chicago's O'Hare airport by FBI agents. He was unarmed and had valid identification. Padilla was not charged with a crime, or with planning a crime. The FBI said he was arrested for "loose talk" about someone at some time detonating a dirty bomb. He was held without access to lawyer or family in a high-security prison in Manhattan. Suddenly, without notification of the court-appointed lawyer, he was moved by the Defense Department to a military brig in North Carolina, where he has been held in solitary confinement, still without access to lawyer or family.[29]

In a rare move, a group of lawyers, federal court judges, district court judges, and bar associations, along with the Cato Institute, the Center for National Security Studies, the Constitution Project, the Lawyers Committee for Human Rights, People for the American Way, and the Rutherford Institute, together issued an amicus brief, making the following statement:

18 U.S.C. [law passed by Congress in 1971 states that] "No citizen shall be . . . detained by the United States except pursuant to an Act of Congress . . . This case involves an unprecedented detention by the U.S. of an American citizen, seized on American soil. And held incommunicado for more than a year without any charge being filed against him, without any access to counsel, and without any right to challenge the basis of this detention before a U.S. judge or magistrate. . . . [We] believe the Executive's position in this case threatens the basic 'rule of law' on which our country is founded, the role of the federal judiciary and the separations in our national government, and fundamental individual liberties enshrined in our Constitution. . . . Throughout history totalitarian regimes have attempted to justify their acts by designating individuals as 'enemies of the state' who were unworthy of any legal rights or protections. These tactics are no less despicable, and perhaps even more so, when they occur in a country that purports to be governed by the rule of law.[30]

4. Section 314 of PATRIOT was used by the FBI to investigate a strip club owner and a numerous politicians for a public corruption probe in Las Vegas.[31]

5. A Canadian citizen was secretly deported to Syria last year by the U.S. government, where he was beaten and tortured for ten months before his release. This was done on a secret presidential "finding" authorizing the CIA to deport foreigners without due process.[32] We have no information concerning how often the government has done this since Mr. Bush and Mr. Ashcroft took office.

6. Members of Congress from both sides of the aisle have complained about the obsession with secrecy regarding the use of the PATRIOT Act by the Bush administration. To make matters worse for those who are concerned about such secrecy, Mr. Ashcroft appeared before the House Judiciary Committee in May of 2003 for the first time since the PATRIOT Act was signed into law. During his appearance, he refused to answer questions put to him on the grounds that "he did not have time."[33]

7. The Cointelpro (counterintelligence program), which spied on Martin Luther King, Jr., Malcolm X, and on war protestors in the 1960's and 1970's, was resurrected by the FBI, in a memo leaked to the New York Times on November 24, 2003.[34]

8. Mr. Ashcroft announced on November 8, 2001, that the Justice Department would begin to listen in on attorney-client phone conversations, where those clients are in federal custody, "including people

who have been detained but not charged with any crime.[35] This includes people being held as "witnesses, detainees, or otherwise." This monitoring will be engaged in without a court order. All that Mr. Ashcroft requires of himself is that he write a letter stating that a "reasonable *suspicion*" (emphasis mine) exists that an inmate *may* use their conversations with an attorney to communicate messages to other terrorists.

This action on the part of the Attorney General can be seen as a direct attack on the Sixth Amendment rights of those arrested. The Sixth Amendment states in part that in all criminal prosecutions, the accused shall enjoy the right to a speedy and public trial, by an impartial jury of the State . . . and to have the assistance of counsel for his defense. How can one have counsel in any meaningful way if the prosecution listens in on attorney-client consultations? The position of the Justice Department here will inevitably result in a situation where the client does not enjoy complete confidentiality with his or her lawyer, thereby affecting the ability of the attorney to create the best defense s/he can for his/her client.

But the Sixth Amendment is not the only applicable one here. This ruling bypasses the Fourth Amendment requirement for probable cause as well. Since the Attorney General can now listen in on attorney-client conversations based on his "suspicion" that something "might" be going on, the process of showing an independent court the reasons for his suspicion is thereby ignored entirely. This is what lawyers refer to as "a fishing expedition," as opposed to the legal warrant application process guaranteed by the Fourth Amendment. Mr. Ashcroft has sought to console those defense lawyers who have objected to his order by telling them that the "taint team," as he calls it, who will listen in on such conversations, will not disclose their evidence to federal prosecutors without the approval of a federal judge first. But in order for this mandate of the Attorney General to produce any investigative fruits, it would have to be shared with other investigators and prosecutors. If not, it is a meaningless rule.

9. President Bush has been busy consolidating power as well. Here are some of his attacks on civil rights.

a. He has publicly stated that he wants administrative subpoenas to replace grand jury subpoenas[36]. This is a key part of Patriot II. Until now, investigators in certain types of cases could obtain administrative subpoenas. But until now, there have been important limits on these types of subpoenas: investigators have been allowed to use them to obtain documents, but not to compel testimony in criminal cases. With this idea of the Executive in mind, a bill called the "Feeney Bill" (from Rep. Tom Feeney, R.-Fla.) has been proposed which would make it illegal for someone to refuse to talk with investigators, whether appealing to the Fifth Amendment or for any other reason. Even more, this bill would give the Justice Department the power to prevent a witness from telling anyone that they received such an administrative subpoena.

          b. On November 13, 2001, President Bush issued a military order regarding the "Detention, Treatment, and Trial of Certain Non-Citizens in the War Against Terrorism."[37] This order takes the entire court system out of the process of arrest and detention of alien terrorist suspects. Equally important, the Sixth Amendment to the U.S. Constitution guaranteeing a trial by jury is dispensed with for immigrants arrested for terrorist activities. The actual statement Mr. Bush makes in this order is as follows:

> The term 'individual subject to this order' shall mean any individual who is not a United States citizen with respect to *whom I determine* . . . that: there is reason to believe that such an individual, at the relevant times . . . [has] as their aim to cause injury to or adverse effects on the United States, its citizens, national security, foreign policy, or economy (emphasis mine).

This definition of "terrorist activity" is very broad and would, of course, include a multitude of crimes that are not necessarily "terrorist" in nature. Once this presidential determination is made, the order directs that federal agents detain that person "at an appropriate location designated by the Secretary of Defense outside or within the United States." Note that the judicial process has been completely circumvented, as the person who is "determined" to have been involved in illegal activity solely by the President, is then held by the Department of Defense. To further underscore the lack of concern for the Fourth Amendment, Mr. Bush continues that the person so arrested shall not be privileged to seek any remedy or maintain any proceeding sought on the individual's behalf in (i) any court of the United States, or any State thereof, (ii) any court of any foreign nation, or (iii) any international tribunal.

          Lest someone declare that this only applies to non-citizens, it is important to note that the Supreme Court has consistently held that the Bill of Rights applies to citizens and non-citizens alike.[38] Furthermore, if the power of the Executive is to be so great that it can deny all rights to immigrants, then it could very well be extended to U.S. persons, such as Patriot II in places does (e.g. loss of natural citizenship and deportation for terrorist related activities). Such shenanigans with the Bill of Rights led the normally conservative editorial writer for the New York Times, William Safire, to accuse Bush of assuming "dictatorial power to ignore our courts." Further, Safire cited the 1866 Supreme Court decision, Ex Parte Milligan, which held both that the Sixth Amendment applied to all persons and cases, and that martial law could not be applied where federal civil courts were still "in business."[39] Safire correctly stated that the United States Code of Military Justice requires that a trial be public, that the proof be beyond a reasonable doubt, that the accused has a say in jury and counsel selection, and that a unanimous verdict be reached (unlike the two-thirds vote ordered by Mr. Bush in the military order). As Safire emphatically claimed: "Not one of those fundamental rights can be found in Bush's military order setting up kangaroo courts for the people he designates before 'trial' to be terrorists."[40]

c. Mr. Bush has ordered what reporters have called "a shadow government" to work outside of Washington D.C., in secret underground sites, without notifying Congress of such a plan. As the Washington Post put it:

> Regardless of whether Bush had an obligation to notify legislative leaders, the congressional leaders' ignorance of the plan he set in motion could raise the question of how this shadow administration would establish its legitimacy with Congress in the event it needed to step in for a crippled White House.[41]

d. The President and his staff have dropped a thick veil of secrecy over the White House, such that information that should and normally would be available is no longer permitted out of the inner circle of the administration. This includes such information as the names and treatment of the prisoners at Guantanamo Bay, the barring of the press and public from immigration hearings, withholding records available under the Freedom of Information Act, and most prominently, the extreme secrecy surrounding the events leading up to 9/11, including the long stonewalling the administration did to prevent an investigation into intelligence and other failures leading to 9/11. Even though Mr. Bush eventually acquiesced to such a panel under political pressure, he continued to stonewall on providing them timely and important information. The attempt to keep this information even from the panel investigating the catastrophe has led many to question the extreme need for Bush secrecy.[42] As Judge Damon Keith said in his ruling against the Bush administration regarding their detention of terrorist suspects, holding them without charge, without access to a lawyer, without disclosing the location of their detention, and incommunicado: "Democracy dies behind closed doors."[43] Disturbingly, this exclusion of all but the administration members from having information includes members of Congress, whom the Bush Whitehouse has told flat out that no more questions from them concerning its spending of taxpayer money will be accepted or answered.[44]

The point here is not to argue that the President, his cabinet, and Congress should not maintain secrets. Especially today, while fighting an elusive and shadowy enemy which has no name or country of origin, certain information needs to be kept from public view. What is disturbing about the Bush administration's secrecy policy, however, is the incredible extent of their secrecy. The Founders of our form of democracy were convinced of the need of an informed electorate. We cannot be informed if every bit of information is withheld from us. Striking the right balance is a tricky thing, but the administration appears to have gone far too far in the direction of not providing even the most basic of information, even concerning information unrelated to its war on terrorism, for the continued smooth functioning of our democratic system. For example, is it really necessary for the war on terrorism that the Bush administration engage in the following acts of secrecy?[45]

1) In the legislation creating the new Department of Homeland Security, the Freedom of Information Act is essentially overturned concerning public health, safety, and environmental issues concerning businesses as well as government. The new legislation forbids disclosure of any information that connects to the "critical infrastructure" that *private industry* labels "sensitive."[46] Thus, businesses are now allowed to conceal even the most minor of safety violations which concern the public health.

2. The Environmental Protection Agency (EPA) and new Department of Homeland Security Director Tom Ridge, were about to embark upon an inspection of the chemical facilities with the worst safety records to insure that they had taken the proper steps to maintain public safety, when suddenly the administration put a stop to it, after intense pressure from the chemical industry. Now the EPA does not even require companies to report the steps they have "voluntarily" undertaken to protect the public health and safety. This is further exacerbated in Patriot II, as we have seen.

3. This penchant for covering their actions with secrecy is not the necessary consequence of the events of 9/11/01. The Bush admini-

stration has been doing this from the day it took office. For example, prior to 9/11, President Bush ordered the following secretive actions:

i. Removal of information from government websites concerning "the use of condoms to prevent HIV/AIDS, the fact that abortions do not increase the risk of breast cancer, Labor Department statistics on mass layoffs, and budget information showing state-by-state cuts in federal programs."[47]

ii. an executive order blocking the release of any presidential record, then the direct order not to release documents from the administration of Ronald Reagan. It is speculated that the reason for this order was to prevent potentially embarrassing information that concerns current administration members from getting out.[48] At any rate, this order violates the 1978 law which ruled that presidential records belong to the public, enacted in response to the attempt by Richard Nixon to do the same thing with his own records.

iii. Vice President Dick Cheney, through most of the Bush administration, has been attempting to block public knowledge of his meeting with energy company lobbyists who were involved with his energy task force. On December 15, the Supreme Court agreed to hear public lawsuits over this issue, but then in June of 2004, ruled in favor of Cheney..

There are numerous other actions the Bush administration has engaged in to prevent the American people from being properly informed. However, the cases listed here should be sufficient to establish that the democratic process is being directly circumvented by the Bush people. Democracy cannot work if the citizens are not informed and able to intelligently debate the major issues of the day. With Bush and Ashcroft putting everything possible under a blanket, including the statue of Lady Justice in the Department of Justice (very symbolic of the administration's attitudes about openness!), they are in effect challenging the very foundations of democracy.

e. The Bush administration has also demonstrated that it is no supporter of dissent or of free expression, when that expression challenges its decisions or its authority. Significantly, the administration has sought to do several things that affect First Amendment rights. First, it has barred demonstrations against Bush policy that take place anywhere near Mr. Bush himself. The administration has set up what they euphemistically call "Free Speech Zones," which are located up to a mile away from where the President travels or speaks. He simply will not acknowledge those who disagree with him. Even more to the point, he is directly attempting to limit the scope and public knowledge of dissent. If informed citizens are the key to the successful functioning of democracy, they need to know both sides to an issue, not just the side the administration wants people to hear. Further, if the administration is to function *democratically*, it must know what **all** of the people have to say, not just the ones who agree with administration viewpoints. Ominously, Brett Bursey, of South Carolina, was arrested for holding a sign along a Bush motorcade route that said "No more war for oil." He was charged with a federal violation of Secret Service restrictions of access to areas close the President. He now faces up to six months in prison and a $5,000 fine. Eleven members of Congress have sent the Attorney General a letter urging him drop the federal prosecution of Bursey. This letter was signed by Ron Paul, Republican Representative from Texas, who said:

> As we read the First Amendment to the Constitution, the United States is a 'free speech zone.' In the United States, free speech is the rule, not the exception, and citizens' rights to express it do not depend on their doing it in a way that the president finds politically amenable.[49]

These and similar cases are being reported around the country.[50]

Another First Amendment issue has arisen with the reintroduction of FBI spying on protesters, ordered by Mr. Ashcroft himself. FBI Intelligence Bulletin no. 89 encourages agents to track how protesters use "the Internet to recruit, raise funds, and coordinate their activities prior to demonstrations," and to "report any potentially illegal acts to the nearest FBI Joint Terrorism Task Force" all under the guise of gaining "current, relevant terrorism information."[51] As a New York Times editorial on this development stated: "The FBI now has nearly unbridled power to poke into the affairs of anyone in the United States, even when there is no evidence of illegal activity."[52] These tactics could well be seen by protesters as attempts at intimidation, or to tacitly persuade potential protesters not to risk speaking their minds for fear of ending up on an FBI list.

While these actions on the part of Ashcroft and the FBI may not in themselves circumvent the First Amendment directly, they do intimidate those who would exercise it to its fullest potential. As Nat Hentoff puts it: "In what part of the Constitution does the FBI have the authority to put in its databases the names of protesters using the Internet to organize peaceful demonstrations?"[53]

VI. Watching our Fears Grow

If what we have reviewed so far is not frightening enough, there is more to be said about the current activities of our government. Anthony Romero has documented at least twenty cases in which citizens and noncitizens alike have been singled out for surveillance by our government already, under the new culture of fear and the USA PATRIOT Act.[54] Among the more famous ones are the government's rounding up over a thousand immigrants immediately after 9/11, holding them without charge and not releasing information on them. Among the more famous individual cases are those of Jose Padilla, and Yasser Esam Hamdi. The lesser-known cases are far greater in number, but rather than detail them each here, perhaps one case cited by Romero will suffice. This case concerns the Denver Police Department monitoring and recording local peaceful protest activities. The targets of such surveillance included a Nobel Peace Prize-winning Quaker organization, the American Friends Service Committee, and a seventy-three-year-old Franciscan nun, Sister Antonia Anthony . . . targets of surveillance also included such notables as former South Dakota Senator James Abourezk . . . George Carlin; Wilma Mankiller, who was awarded the Medal of Freedom, the nation's highest civilian honor...and historian Vine Deloria.[55]

The ACLU filed a class-action lawsuit, which resulted in the Denver City Council adopting a resolution reaffirming an existing ordinance that bars Denver City Police from investigating and collecting information on citizens on the basis of their First Amendment activities.

Romero also documents that the same type of activity on the part of government officials is now occurring in such states as Louisiana, Virginia, Florida, and Maryland, all of which have passed bills that allow for expanded governmental surveillance powers concerning their citizens.

We should also note the rather ominous comments made by Supreme Court Justice Sandra Day O'Connor during her visit to Ground Zero in New York City, that Americans are likely to see "more restrictions on personal freedom than has ever been the case in this country."[56]

Finally, we must note the proposal of the Bush administration to standardize all state drivers' licenses, and to keep all information related to it on file in a central government computer base. This would create "a de facto national I.D. card," warns Romero, which "would almost certainly become the repositories of extensive personal information, which could be easily accessed and abused."[57]

VII. Final Reflections

Do all of the actions of the Bush administration we have seen in this book mean that America is becoming a police state? Perhaps the decisive evidence in answering this question will come with a brief examination of the role of the U.S. military in domestic affairs.

One of the first things that must be noted with regard to the military being used domestically with local law enforcement comes in the form of a message from Deputy Defense Secretary Paul Wolfowitz, who submitted in testimony to Congress that it is time for them to reexamine the Posse Comitatus Act of 1878, which forbids the U.S. military from doing domestic law enforcement.[58] Since then the news media has reported that massive amounts of federal subsidies are being funneled to local law enforcement officials for intelligence operations. With the PATRIOT Act having taken down the walls between prosecution and intelligence, any information collected by local law enforcement is passed along to the feds, with federal tax money given to local police to engage in such information gathering.

Furthermore, the U.S. military is in fact assisting local police agencies with both intelligence gathering and law enforcement. Air Force General Ralph E. Eberhart, among others, has been making the public case that the military needs to start focusing on "the home game" regarding terrorism. William Arkin of the Los Angeles Times has written that such actions are breaking down the traditional barriers to military action and surveillance within the United States itself, all under the guise of terrorism. Even though today we see such use of the military on citizens, it must be noted that this did not start with the war on terrorism, but has been coming for nearly ten years. Arkin accurately stated the trend toward military enforcement of domestic federal government laws in the following way:

> amendments approved by Congress in 1996 for that earlier civilian war, the war on drugs, have already expanded the military's domestic powers so that Washington can act unilaterally in dispatching the military without waiting for a state's request for help. Long before 9/11, Congress authorized the military to assist local law enforcement officials in domestic 'drug interdiction' and during terrorist incidents involving weapons of mass destruction.[59]

If these legal permissions were not enough for the military to enter into domestic affairs, consider the what has been reported during the Free Trade Association (FTAA) meeting in Miami in late November, 2003. All Miami police chief John Timoney needed to do to obtain

$8.5 billion in federal funds for "security" during the summit was to classify the protesters as "outsiders coming in to terrorize the city."[60] Once the magic word "terrorize" was used, the funds and the feds came pouring into Miami. Even more disturbing are the reports from this meeting which describe the "extreme force" used by Miami police in dealing with otherwise peaceful protesters.[61]

These are surely telling signs that the military apparatus, including the intelligence-gathering arms of the federal government, are now starting to be aimed directly at citizens in this country, with the cooperation of local police departments. There is almost certainly more of this to come in future years. It is something that every citizen should be informed of and regarding which every U.S. person should be very wary and questioning.

In addition to the incursion of the military into local police law enforcement and intelligence gathering, it is important to note that one of the main presuppositions behind the passage of the PATRIOT Act, and one that continues to hold sway with legislators today, is the belief that more federal authority, and more surveillance of and reduced rights for U.S. persons, is a way to ensure fewer terrorist activities. But there are several serious flaws to this philosophy. First of all, it is unclear how the federal government can really protect the country by preventing terrorist attacks to begin with. This is a far more difficult task than a local police department protecting its citizenry from would-be criminals by preventing those criminal actions from taking place. Terrorist attacks, as we have seen, originate from small cadres of persons whose actions are unpredictable. If there is no way for the police department to stop all or even most crimes from taking place, there is no way for the federal government to prevent terrorist attacks completely.

Second, it is manifestly unclear precisely how it can be the case that more federal power in the form of reduced civil rights for citizens results in greater national security. This is a key presumption behind PATRIOT and the other pieces of legislation covered in this book. Not only is there little cogent support to such a presupposition, but the failures of current intelligence apparatuses that were in place at the time of 9/11/01 were far more at fault in allowing the events of that day to occur than was the lack of power and knowledge of the federal government about the daily activities of its citizens. Those who support PATRIOT and other legislation to give more power to the federal government fail to account for the fact that the government failed horrendously to use the power they *already* had in ways that would have protected American lives on 9/11. Some instances of misused power can be put in the form of questions. For example, why did Mr. Ashcroft and other Pentagon officials switch to chartered flights prior to 9/11? What did Mr. Bush know in his Presidential Daily Brief regarding the coming attack from al-Qaeda? David Corn, in the Los Angeles Weekly, says the July 2001 intelligence warning that was sent to Mr. Bush said: "We believe that [bin Laden] will launch a significant terrorist attack against the U.S. and/or Israeli interests in the coming weeks."[62] Further, on August 6, Mr. Bush was again advised by National Security Advisor Condoleeza Rice that bin Laden was planning a major attack against the U.S. Why was nothing done to investigate this and/or take preventive action concerning it, other than administration officials ceasing to use commercial flights? Why did the FBI not do anything when its own agents Colleen Rowley and others attempted repeatedly to warn that suspected al-Qaeda operatives were taking flying lessons and could use planes to attack America? Why did NORAD take twenty-five minutes to discover that planes had been hijacked? Why were members of the Saudi Arabian government permitted to fly home from the U.S. after the attacks of 9/11, while flying was still prohibited to American citizens? Why did the administration lie about the role of Saddam Hussein in the attacks? Why did it lie about the health risks involved in letting people return to Wall Street and the area surrounding the World Trade Center when the EPA reports concluded that there were still significant health risks involved to the public from asbestos dust and other toxins still in the air from the collapse of the towers?[63] When these and other considerations are taken into account, it hardly seems that the way to prevent future terrorist attacks is to give more power to the very people who egregiously failed to use it to protect American lives. Besides, we have taken the course for years, now, of giving the federal government more power, and we are still being attacked by terrorists. Perhaps it is time to try an alternative to power-enhancement and rights-reduction.

Again, consider the fact that not one of the persons involved in 9/11 was a U.S. citizen. Even in the single case of domestic terrorism on record, that of Timothy McVeigh and Terry Nichols bombing the Oklahoma City Federal Building, it would be difficult to maintain that the federal or state government would have been able to prevent such an occurrence if they had more information taken from the electronic correspondence of McVeigh and Nichols. Even if such a case could be made, at what expense, in terms of lost civil rights, would such an ability be secured? Furthermore, to truncate civil rights for the sake of protecting them is an irresolvable contradiction. Once rights are gone or substantially reduced, how are they to being thereby "protected"? Even more, once gone or reduced, how are they to be recovered? Will the government willingly and pleasurably return rights to their current standing once they have put into place vast resources of gathering information on and power over U.S. citizens? The chances seem rather slim that this will happen. Furthermore, if we accept the governmental claim that it is necessary to truncate rights for the sake of fighting the war on terrorism, when would such a war conceivably end? Since there are literally countless terrorist "cells," since there is no way to find out who "they" all are, since they operate in deep secrecy while simultaneously having no country of origin or support and no centralized leader, and since they strike without warning and without geographical origin, this "war" that "necessitates" limitation or surrender of rights very well could be an endless state of war. No, it seems as though fighting a shadowy enemy with no known location or pattern, and without having to necessarily and extensively use contemporary communication devices, would cause far too many of our current rights to be severely restricted, if not eliminated, in order to chase these shadows. And what degree of success could this procedure guarantee or even predict? Certainly taking away civil rights will not put a stop to terrorist activities. On the other hand, if we reduce or eliminate citizen rights and liberties, the terrorists will have succeeded at bringing down American democracy. At a time when democracy is under attack, the last thing it would be prudent to do is to attack democracy from within by consolidating federal power over the lives of its citizens and denying citizens rights to information, free speech, privacy, etc.

So what positive steps could we take, outside of granting the government more power over our lives, to reduce the chances of future terrorist attacks? I say "reduce" because to "eliminate" them is as impossible as eliminating crime itself.

First of all, preserving what is essential to democracy, our rights, becomes all the more critical when they are being attacked from outside of that tradition (i.e. by al Qaeda or others who would seek to put an end to such an "open" form of government). Most importantly, the idea of universal "liberty" is the defining moment of American democracy. Without a presupposition of liberty for the people, democracy is perverted into something else. As we saw in Chapter One, Liberty is the most important, most prominent natural right of persons, according to our "intellectual father," John Locke. It includes, as we have seen, the right not to be interfered with as we pursue our own "innocent ends." This right includes the right to privacy, as we have also seen. To lose or otherwise subdue or destroy this individual liberty to live unhampered by and unafraid of our government would be to lose sight of what really makes our country great. It is even more reprehensible that the Bush administration has chosen to play on fear as a means of abstracting power from the people. A far more effective tool to fight terrorism would be to stand united, firm and public in our commitment to uphold liberty and its foundations, since that is part of what is being attacked when terrorists strike.

Second, when legislation of any sort, from that of Congress to that of a presidential executive order, seeks to curtail general liberties or specific constitutional rights, citizens and conscientious leaders should sound alarms. Locke says that when there is a distinct pattern of power-grabbing and liberty-reducing actions on the part of a government, that government ceases to work for the people. As he so poignantly stated this issue, "the end of law is not to abolish or restrain, but to preserve and enlarge freedom." When the actions and ends of government do the former instead of the latter, that government has ceased to act as a democratic one. It is the contention of this author that this is precisely what is happening at this time in America. Thus, people need to start speaking out against creeping and creepy government usurpation of powers unnecessary to their mandate to protect their citizens.

Furthermore, as Locke rightly maintains, in a democratic form of government, even with powerful rulers of legislative and executive branches, "there remains still in the people a Supream Power to remove or alter the Legislative."[64] The Founders of American democracy were so keenly aware of this need to keep the people as the main focus and thus keep governmental power in check that they instituted a third branch, the judicial, to keep power separated. This is precisely what is being overrun, or rather, done an end-run around, in the PATRIOT Act and its siblings, along with other actions undertaken by the Bush administration, as noted herein.

Third, examination of U.S. foreign policy and involvements, such as the carte blanche support for Israel, might be a far more effective remedy for the U.S. vulnerability to terrorist activity than to turn our democracy into a national security state reminiscent of the old Soviet Union.

Fourth, a foreign policy that seeks to *allow* (not to force through military might) the extension of the rights we say we hold sacred, to all segments of the globe would be one that would elicit less response by terrorist attack than one which seeks economic, military, or political hegemony on foreign soils and peoples, which is arguably what current U.S. foreign policy has been about for the last twenty-five years or more. A politics of "inclusion" of all those with a voice is a better option than fighting every segment of every society in order that we may have "our way" in the world.

The argument made in this text, and particularly in this chapter, has been that there is no dilemma between liberty and security, because the USA PATRIOT Act and its successors do not make an argument for, nor are they directed at, more security from terrorists. Rather, they are power-enhancing and liberty-reducing Acts (e.g. "suspicion" replaces probable cause; "criminal activity" replaces "terrorist activity;" no judiciary, or reduced judiciary, etc.). Furthermore, those who would attempt to argue that more security either requires or is a necessary consequence of less liberty fail to explain not only how these two categories are so inversely related, but in fact fail to explain how systematically undermining our democratic heritage in the form of the Bill of Rights, preserves it. Perhaps Benjamin Franklin put it best when he said: "They that can give up essential liberty to obtain a little temporary safety deserve neither liberty nor safety."

Notes

1 Locke, *Second Treatise*, Chapter III, paragraph 17.
2 Reuters, July 22. 2003.
3 These items were compiled from information taken from http://slate.msn.com.
4 www.aclu.org, November 5, 2003.
5 Ibid.
6 Lobe, Jim. "Patriot Act Expansion Moves Through Congress," *OneWorld US*, November 21, 2003.
7 ACLU, "Stop the Expanded Use of Secret Searches," www.aclu.org, November 13, 2003.
8 Ibid.
9 The following items were taken from Nancy Chang, "How Democracy Dies: The War on Our Civil Liberties," in Cynthia Brown, ed. *Lost Liberties: Ashcroft and the Assault on Personal Freedom* (New York: The New Press, 2003), pp. 34-35 & 48-49.
10 See Chang, ibid., p. 37.
11 For details on this assertion, see Reg Whitaker, "After 9/11: A Surveillance State?" in ibid., pages 52-71.
12 Ibid., p. 55.
13 For example, see the USA PATRIOT Act, Sections 216, 218, and 225.
14 Whitaker, op. cit., p. 62.
15 Schmitt, Richard B. "Patriot Act Author Has Concerns," *Los Angeles Times*, November 30, 2003.
16 http://aclu.org.
17 *The Washington Post*, August 8, 2003.
18 Ibid.
19 Reuters, July 30, 2003. See also *The Diane Rehm* show, op. cit., August 20, 2003.
20 *The Associated Press*, December 19, 2003.
21 The Daily Southtown, October 2, 2003; reprinted in Common Dreams Newsletter, October 2, 2003.
22 *Christian Science Monitor*, September 16, 2003; *The New York Times*, September 8, 2003.
23 *The Washington Post*, May 21, 2003; New York Times, Sept. 27, 2003
24 *The New York Times*, May 30, 2003
25 *The New York Times*, August 23, 2002.
26 *Christian Science Monitor*, Sept. 16, 2003
27 *Chicago Tribune*, Editorial page, Sept. 21, 2003
28 Ibid.
29 *The Village Voice*, September 19, 2003.
30 Ibid.

31 Kalil, J.M., and Steve Tetreault, "PATRIOT ACT: Law's Use Causing Concerns," *Las Vegas Review-Journal*, November 5, 2003.

32 Brown, DeNeen L. and Dana Priest, "Deported Terror Suspect Details Torture in Syria," *Washington Post*, November 5, 2003.

33 "Ashcroft Defends Detentions as Immigrants Recount Toll," *The New York Times*, May 5, 2003.

34 Rothschild, Matthew. "Ashcroft's Cointelpro," *The Progressive*, November 24, 2003.

35 See Lardner, George, Jr. "U.S. Will Monitor Calls to Lawyers," *Washington Post*, November 9, 2001.

36 *Washington Post*, Sept. 13, 2003

37 Available at whitehouse.gov.

38 See *Zadvydas v. Davis*, 121 S. Ct. 2491, 2500 (2001) (quoted in Chang, "The USA PATRIOT Act," op. cit.). A detailed analysis of this military order by the President is done in Lynch, Timothy. "Breaking the Vicious Cycle: Preserving Our Liberties While Fighting Terrorism," *Policy Analysis*, no. 443, June 26, 2002.

39 For more detail on *Ex Parte Mulligan*, see ibid.

40 Safire, William. "Kangaroo Courts," *Truthout*, November 26, 2001.

41 Goldstein, Amy, and Juliet Eilperin. "Congress Not Advised of Shadow Government," *Washington Post*, March 2, 2002. See also Gellman, Barton, and Susan Schmidt. "Shadow Government Is at Work in Secret," *Washington Post*, March 1, 2002. The latter article was the one that "broke" the story.

42 For more information on Bush secrecy, especially with issues related to 9/11/01, see "9/11 Commission Chairman: White House Withholding 9/11 Documents," *Reuters*, October 26, 2003. See also the following: "9/11 Victims' Relatives: Extend Probe," *Associated Press*, November 26, 2003; Philip Shenon, "Administration Faces Subpoenas From 9/11 Panel," *New York Times*, October 25, 2003; Tim Harper, "What Did Bush Know Before 9/11 Attacks?," *The Toronto Star*, November 15, 2003; William Bunch, "What Don't We Have Answers to These 9/11 Questions?," *The Philadelphia Daily News*, September 11, 2003; David Corn, "The 9/11 Cover-up." *Los Angeles Weekly*, November 21, 2003; Philip Shenon, "Panel Reaches Deal on Access to 9/11 Papers," *New York Times*, November 13, 2003; "The Fruits of Secrecy," *New York Times* editorial, November 8, 2003 (concerning Bush secrecy regarding environmental regulations and Environmental Protection Agency rulings).

43 For more on the issue of Bush administration secrecy, see Nancy Chang, *Silencing Political Dissent*, chapters 3 and 4; Richard C. Leone, *The War on Our Freedoms*, chapter 9; C. William Michaels, *No Greater Threat*, Part V. The New York Times has also done a multitude of articles during the past year on Bush-Ashcroft secrecy: see especially Paul Krugman writings.

44 Milbank, Dana. "White House Puts Limits on Queries From Democrats," *The Washington Post*, November 9, 2003.

45 The following examples are taken from John Podesta, "Need to Know: Governing in Secret," in Richard C. Leone, *The War on Our Freedoms*, op. cit., Chapter 9.

46 Ibid., p. 227.

47 Ibid., p. 230.

48 This is Podesta's assertion, ibid.

49 Levendosky, Charles, "Keeping Protesters Out of Sight and Out of Hearing," *International Herald Tribune*, November 7, 2003.

50 For more on this, see Nancy Chang, *Silencing Political Dissent*, Chapter Four, op. cit.

51 Quotes in Hentoff, Nat. "J. Edgar Hoover Back at the 'New' FBI," *The Village Voice*, December 4, 2003.

52 Ibid.

53 Ibid.

54 Anthony D. Romero, "Living in Fear: How the U.S. Government's War on Terror Impacts American Lives," in Cynthia Brown, op. cit., pp. 112-131.

55 Ibid., p. 125.

56 Greenhouse, Linda. "In New York Visit, O'Connor Foresees Limits on Freedom," *The New York Times*, September 29, 2001.

57 Ibid., p. 127. See also William Safire, "Threat of National ID," New York Times, December 24, 2001.

58 Loeb, Vernon. "Review of Military's Domestic Role Urged," *Washington Post*, October 5, 2001.

59 Arkin, William. "Mission Creep Hits Home," *Los Angeles Times*, November 23, 2003. See also Naomi Klein, "America's Enemy Within," *The Guardian*, November 26, 2003.

60 Klein, ibid.

61 Ibid. See also Rachel La Corte, "Protesters Say Miami Police Abused Them," *Associated Press*, November 25, 2003.

62 Corn, op. cit.

63 For these and numerous other questions the Bush administration has refused to answer, see Tim Harper, "What Did Bush Know Before the 9/11 Attacks?" *The Toronto Star*, op. cit.

64 Ibid., Chapter XIII, paragraph 149.

Bibliography

American Civil Liberties Union. "ACLU Slams Classified FBI Memorandum Directing Law Enforcement to Engage in Protest Suppression Tactics," www.aclu.org, November 23, 2003.

American Civil Liberties Union. "Stop the Expanded Use of Secret Searches," www.aclu.org, November 13, 2003.

American Civil Liberties Union Question and Answer Sheet on the Pentagon's "Total Information Awareness." www.aclu.org.

American Civil Liberties Union. "Total Information Compliance: The TIA's Burden Under the Wyden Amendment," www.aclu.org.

Anonymous. criticisms of "Patriot II:" www.foi.missouri.edu; www.aclu.org; www.ratical.org

Anonymous. "Your Right to Privacy," www.rightotprivacy.com.

Arkin, William M. "Mission Creep Hits Home," *Los Angeles Times*, November 23, 2003.

Ashcroft, John, et. al. Justice Department response to criticisms of the USA PATRIOT Act, www.lifeandliberty.gov

The Associated Press. "9/11 Victims' Relatives: Extend Probe," November 26, 2003.

Balkin, Jack M. "USA PATRIOT Act: A Dreadful Act II," *Los Angeles Times*, February 13, 2003.

Bamford, James. "Washington Bends the Rules," *The New York Times*, August 27, 2002.

Braman, Chuck. "The Political Philosophy of John Locke and Its Influence on the Founding Fathers and the Political Documents They Created," www.chuckbraman.com/writing, 1996.

Brown, Cynthia. *Lost Liberties: Ashcroft and the Assault on Personal Freedom.* New York: The New Press, 2003.

Brown, DeNeen L., and Dana Priest. "Deported Terror Suspect Details Torture in Syria," *The Washington Post*, November 5, 2003.

Bunch, William. "Why Don't We Have Answers to These 9/11 Questions?," *The Philadelphia Daily News*, September 11, 2003.

Chang, Nancy. *Silencing Political Dissent* New York: Seven Stories Press, 2002.

Chang,, Nancy. "The USA PATRIOT Act: What's So Patriotic About Trampling on the Bill of Rights?" at www.ccr-ny.org/whatsnew/usa_patriot_act.asp.

C-SPAN. "PATRIOT Act Hearing in the Senate Judiciary Committee," 10/21/03.

Chicago Tribune editorial. "Security and Liberty in the Balance," June 9, 2003.

Chicago Tribune editorial. "Protecting Rights in Time of War," November 2, 2003.

Chicago Tribune editorial. "Myth, Reality and the Patriot Act," November 5, 2003.

Chicago Tribune editorial. "Tearing Down Intelligence Walls," November 9, 2003.

Chicago Tribune editorial. "Paring Back the Patriot Act," November 12, 2003.

Chicago Tribune editorial. "Prisoners in the War on Terror," November 16, 2003.

Chicago Tribune editorial. "John Ashcroft's Problem," November 19, 2003.

Chicago Tribune editorial. "Securing a Free Nation," November 23, 2003.

Clark, Andrew. "House Takes Aim at Patriot Act Secret Searches," *Reuters*, July 22, 2003.

Cohen, Patricia. "9/11 Law Means More Snooping? Or Maybe Less?" *The New York Times*, September 7, 2002.

Cole, David. *Enemy Aliens.* New York: The New Press, 2003.

Cole, David and James X. Dempsey. *Terrorism and the Constitution.* New York: The New Press, 2002.

Corn, David. "The 9/11 Cover-up," *Los Angeles Weekly*, November 21, 2003.

Cronkite, Walter. "The New Inquisition," *The Denver Post*, September 21, 2003.

Dobberstein, John. "Chicago City Council Chides Patriot Act," *The Daily Southtown*, October 2. 2003.

Dowd, Maureen. "Scaring Up Votes," *The New York Times*, November 23, 2003.

Edgar, Timothy H. "Section-by-Section Analysis of the Justice Department Draft 'Domestic Security Enhancement Act of 2003,' also known as 'PATRIOT Act II," www.aclu.org/news, February 14, 2003.

Eggen Dan. "GOP Bill Would Add Anti-Terror Powers," *The Washington Post*, August 21, 2003.

———. "Patriot Act Faces New Challenge in Court," *The Washington Post*, August 6, 2003.

———. "Patriot Act Use Expands," *The Washington Post*, May 21, 2003.

Fainaru, Steve, and James V. Grimaldi. "FBI Knew Terrorists Were Using Flight School," *The Washington Post*, September 23, 2001.

Fine, Glenn A. "Excerpt From Analysis of Detention of Foreigners After 9/11," *The New York Times*, June 3, 2003.

Gellman, Barton, and Susan Schmidt. "Shadow Government is at Work in Secret," *The Washington Post*, March 1, 2002.

Goldstein, Amy. "The Patriot Act: Fierce Fight Over Secrecy, Scope of Law," *The Washington Post*, September 8, 2003.

Harper, Tim. "What Did Bush Know Before 9/11 Attacks?," *The Toronto Star*, November 14, 2003.

Hentoff, Nat. "Bush Accused By Lords of the Bar," *The Village Voice*, September 19, 2003.

———. "J. Edgar Hoover Back at the 'New' FBI," *The Village Voice*, December 4, 2003.

———. *The War on the Bill of Rights and the Gathering Resistance.* New York: Seven Stories Press, 2003.

Herbert, Bob. "Secrecy is Our Enemy," *The New York Times*, September 2, 2002.

Hicks, John D., George E. Mowry, and Robert E. Burke. A History of American Democracy Boston: Houghton Mifflin, 1970.

Isilkoff, Michael. "Show Me the Money," *Newsweek*, December 1, 2003.

Kalil, J.M., and Steve Tetreault. "PATRIOT ACT: Law's Use Causing Concerns," *Las Vegas Review-Journal*, November 5, 2003.

Klein, Naomi. "America's Enemy Within," *The Guardian*, November 26, 2003.

Lacayo, Richard. "The War Comes Back Home," *Time Magazine*, May 4, 2003.

Lardner, George, Jr. "U.S. Will Monitor Calls to Lawyers," *Washington Post*, November 9, 2001.

Leone, Richard C. and Greg Anrig, Jr. *The War on Our Freedoms.* New York: PublicAffairs, 2003.

Lewis, Anthony. "Taking Our Liberties," *The New York Times*, March 9, 2002.

Lewis, Charles, and Adam Mayle. "Justice Department Drafts Sweeping Expansion of Anti-Terrorism Act," Center for Public Integrity. www.publicintegrity.org.

Levendosky, Charles. "Keeping the Protestors Out of Sight and Out of Hearing," *International Herald Tribune*, November 6, 2003. Republished in *Common Dreams Newsletter*, November 7, 2003.

Levy, Leonard. *Origins of the Bill of Rights*. New Haven: Yale University Press, 1999.

Lichtblau, Eric. "Bush Seeks to Expand Access to Private Data," *The New York Times*, September 14, 2003.

Lichtblau, Eric. "Plans for Terror Inquiries Still Fall Short, Report Says," *The New York Times*, September 9, 2003.

———. "Republicans Want Terror Law Made Permanent," *The New York Times*, April 9, 2003.

———. "U.S. Report Faults the Roundup of Illegal Immigrants After 9/11," *The New York Times*, June 3, 2003.

———. "U.S. Will Tighten Rules on Holding Terror Suspects," *The New York Times*, June 13, 2003.

———. "Ashcroft's Tour Rallies Supporters and Detractors," *The New York Times*, September 8, 2003.

———. "Suit Challenges Constitutionality of Powers in Antiterrorism Law," *The New York Times*, July 21, 2003.

———. "U.S. Uses Terror Law to Pursue Crimes From Drugs to Swindling," *The New York Times*, September 27, 2003.

———. "U.S. Cautiously Begins to Seize Millions in Foreign Banks," *The New York Times*, May 30, 2003.

———. "F.B.I. Scrutinizes Antiwar Rallies," *The New York Times*, November 23, 2003.

Liptak, Adam. "Court Backs Open Deportation Hearings in Terror Cases," *The New York Times*, August 27, 2002.

Lobe, Jim. "New Activist Network Slams Growing Abuses Under Bush," *Inter Press Service News Agency*, December 11, 2003.

————. "Patriot Act Expansion Moves Through Congress," *OneWorld US*, November 21, 2003.

Loeb, Vernon. "Review of Military's Domestic Role Urged," *Washington Post*, October 5, 2001.

Locke, John. *Two Treatises of Government*, edited with an Introduction by Peter Laslett. Cambridge: Cambridge University Press, 1988.

Lynch, Timothy. "Breaking the Vicious Cycle: Preserving Our Liberties While Fighting Terrorism," *Policy Analysis*, No. 443, June 26, 2002.

McGee, Jim. "In Federal Law Enforcement, 'All the Walls are Down'." *Washington Post*, October 14, 2003.

Michaels, C. William. *No Greater Threat: America After September 11 and the Rise of a National Security State*. New York: Algora Publishing, 2002.

Milbank, Dana. "White House Puts Limits on Queries From Democrats," *The Washington Post*, November 8, 2003.

Monk, Linda. *The Bill of Rights: A User's Guide*. Close Up Publishing, 1995.

Monk, Linda. *The Words We Live By*. New York: Hyperion, 2003.

Murray, Frank J. "Patriot Act of 2001 Casts Wide Net," *The Washington Times*, June 16, 2003.

New York Times editorial. "The Fruits of Secrecy," November 8, 2003.

National Security Enhancement Act of 2003 ("Patriot II"). www.publicintegrity.org

O'Neil, Brigid. "The PATRIOT Act's Assault on the Bill of Rights," The Independent Institute, www.independent.org/tii/news. September 15, 2003.

Parrish, Geov. "The Police State Enhancement Act of 2003," The Freedom of Information Center. www.foi.missouri.edu.

Presidential military order. www.whitehouse.gov. "Presidential Issues Military Order," November 13, 2001.

Regan, Tom. "Ashcroft Slams Critics as Patriot Act Backlash Grows," Christian Science Monitor, September 16, 2003.

Rehm, Diane. "The Diane Rehm Show: The PATRIOT Act," WAMU, American University, Washington, D.C., August 20, 2003.

Reuters. "9/11 Commission Chairman: White House Withholding 9/11 Documents," October 26, 2003.

Richey, Warren. "Secret 9/11 Case Before High Court," *The Christian Science Monitor*, October 30, 2003.

Rothschild, Matthew. "Ashcroft's Cointelpro," *The Progressive*, November 24, 2003.

Safire, William. "Kangaroo Courts," *Truthout*, November 26, 2001.

———. "Threat of National ID," *New York Times* editorial, December 24, 2001.

Savage, Charlie. "Patriot Act Hearings Sought by Democrats," *The Boston Globe*, December 12, 2003.

Schmitt, Richard B. "Patriot Act Author Has Concerns," *Los Angeles Times*, November 30, 2003.

Shachtman, Noah. "The Pentagon's Plan for Tracking Everything That Moves," *The Village Voice*, July 9, 2003.

Shapiro, Ian. *The Evolution of Rights in Liberal Theory.* Cambridge: Cambridge University Press, 1986.

Shenon, Philip. "Administration Faces Subpoenas From 9/11 Panel," *New York Times*, October 25, 2003.

———. "Panel Reaches Deal on Access to 9/11 Papers," *The New York Times*, November 13, 2003.

———. "Secret Court Says F.B.I. Aides Misled Judges in 75 Cases," *The New York Times*, August 23, 2002.

Simmons, A. John. *The Lockean Theory of Rights*. Princeton, New Jersey: Princeton University Press, 1992.

Swarns, Rachel L. "Illegal Aliens Can Be Held Indefinitely, Ashcroft Says," *The New York Times*, April 26, 2003.

Taylor, Guy. "Communities Shun Patriot Act," *The Washington Times*, July 21, 2003.

Tribe, Laurence H. "Citizens, Combatants, and the Constitution," *The New York Times*, June 16, 2002.

USA Patriot Act. www.epic.org/privacy/terrorism/usapatriot

Van Bergen, Jennifer. "Repeal the USA Patriot Act," *Truthout.org*, April 1, 2002.

Washington Post editorial. "Liberty Bushwhacked," September 13, 2003.

Index